Fodor's
Pocket
London

S0-BOB-316

Reprinted from Fodor's *Great Britain 2000*

Fodor's Travel Publications, Inc.
New York • Toronto • London • Sydney • Auckland
www.fodors.com

Fodor's Pocket London

Editors: Robert I.C. Fisher, Lauren A. Myers
Editorial Contributors: Jacqueline Brown, Lucy Hawking, Kate Sekules
Editorial Production: Nicole Revere
Maps: David Lindroth Inc., *cartographer*; Rebecca Baer and Robert Blake, *map editors*
Design: Fabrizio La Rocca, *creative director*; Guido Caroti, *art director*
Production/Manufacturing: Mike Costa
Cover Photograph: Brian Yarvin/Peter Arnold, Inc.

Copyright

ISBN 0–679–00349–5
ISSN 1094–7124

Special Sales

Fodor's Travel Publications are available at special discounts for bulk purchases for sales promotions or premiums. Special editions, including personalized covers, excerpts of existing guides, and corporate imprints, can be created in large quantities for special needs. For more information, contact your local bookseller or write to Special Markets, Fodor's Travel Publications, 201 East 50th Street, New York, NY 10022. Inquiries from Canada should be directed to your local Canadian bookseller or sent to Random House of Canada, Ltd., Marketing Department, 2775 Matheson Boulevard East, Mississauga, Ontario L4W 4P7. Inquiries from the United Kingdom should be sent to Fodor's Travel Publications, 20 Vauxhall Bridge Road, London SW1V 2SA, England.

PRINTED IN THE UNITED STATES OF AMERICA

10 9 8 7 6 5 4 3 2 1

Important Tip

Although all prices, opening times, and other details in this book are based on information supplied to us at press time, changes occur all the time in the travel world, and Fodor's cannot accept responsibility for facts that become outdated or for inadvertent errors or omissions. So **always confirm information when it matters,** especially if you're making a detour to visit a specific place.

CONTENTS

Maps

ON THE ROAD WITH FODOR'S

EVERY Y2K TRIP is a significant trip. So if there was ever a time you needed excellent travel information, it's now. Acutely aware of that fact, we've pulled out all stops in preparing *Fodor's Pocket London 2000*. To guide you in putting together your British experience, we've created itineraries and neighborhood walks. And to direct you to the places that are truly worth your time and money in this important year, we've rallied the team of endearingly picky know-it-alls we're pleased to call our writers. Having seen all corners of London, they're real experts. If you knew them, you'd poll them for tips yourself.

Since **Kate Sekules** lives with a foot on either side of the Atlantic, her mission is getting the best of both worlds—and Fodor's is much the winner. Thanks to her knack for coming up with the telling phrase, her wit is much in demand: *Vogue, W, Travel Holiday, Harper's Bazaar, Travel & Leisure,* and *The New Yorker* are just some of the publications she writes for. Happily, she found enough time to do much of the writing for this guidebook (several editions later, now somewhat revised). She is currently travel editor at *Food & Wine*.

Being a settler in London, says writer and editor **Jacqueline Brown,** is mainly different from being a true native in that one really tries to get the most out of what the city has to offer. After 20 years of living in the capital, her favorite targets are those culinary and cultural arenas which lie far beyond bully beef and Buckingham Palace. When she is not working as a freelance editor or helping to update the Destination: London, Exploring, Dining, Shopping, Side Trips, and Smart Travel Tips sections of this book, Jacqueline can be found strolling the parklands of a National Trust stately home with her young family.

From running a business newspaper in Prague to repossessing cars (for a magazine story) in the Bronx, **Lucy Hawking**'s career has certainly been unpredictable. A trilingual Oxford graduate, she has flitted around the globe, writing for several London and New York publications. But now, thanks to the arrival of a handsome baby boy, she has settled in London where she works for the *Times* and has helped us update the Exploring, Lodging, Nightlife and the Arts, and Outdoor Activities and Sports sections. She recently found that loading the car with diapers and other baby-related items for a trip through the Thames Valley was rather different from hopping on a plane with just a credit card. Baby William was especially impressed by the magnificence of Blenheim Palace—perhaps he felt it was more his style than an apartment in London.

Editor **Robert I. C. Fisher,** weaned on a steady diet of Masterpiece Theater productions, remains convinced that every word uttered with an English accent is a pearl. After working on three other Fodor's guidebooks to Great Britain and London, he knows that if Dickens had used a PC for his wordy tomes he would have had a mean case of carpal tunnel syndrome. A raging Anglophile, Robert believes Queen Vicky was the true author of *Alice's Adventures in Wonderland*. Along the way, he's written on a variety of Europe-based subjects for such magazines as *Town & Country* and *Art in America*.

Don't Forget to Write

Keeping a travel guide fresh and up-to-date is a big job. So we love your feedback—positive and negative—and follow up on all suggestions. Contact the Pocket London editor at editors@fodors.com or c/o Fodor's, 201 East 50th Street, New York, New York 10022. And have a wonderful trip!

Karen Cure
Editorial Director

SMART TRAVEL TIPS

AIR TRAVEL

➤ MAJOR AIRLINES: **American Airlines** (☎ 800/433–7300, 020/8572–5555 in London) to Heathrow, Gatwick. **British Airways** (☎ 800/247–9297, 0345/222–1111 in London) to Heathrow, Gatwick. **Continental** (☎ 800/231–0856, 0800/776464 in London) to Gatwick. **Delta** (☎ 800/241–4141, 0800/414767 in London) to Gatwick. **Northwest Airlines** (☎ 800/447–4747, 0990/561000 in London) to Gatwick. **United** (☎ 800/241–6522, 0845/844–4777 in London) to Heathrow. **TWA** (☎ 800/892–4141, 020/8814–0707 in London) to Gatwick. **Virgin Atlantic** (☎ 800/862–8621, 01293/747747 in London) to Heathrow, Gatwick.

➤ CONSOLIDATORS: **Cheap Tickets** (☎ 800/377–1000). **Discount Airline Ticket Service** (☎ 800/576–1600). **Unitravel** (☎ 800/325–2222). **Up & Away Travel** (☎ 212/889–2345). **World Travel Network** (☎ 800/409–6753).

FLYING TIMES

Flying time to London is about 6½ hours from New York, 7½ hours from Chicago, and 10 hours from Los Angeles.

AIRPORTS & TRANSFERS

International flights to London arrive at either **Heathrow Airport,** 15 mi west of London, or at **Gatwick Airport,** 27 mi south of the capital. Most flights from the United States go to Heathrow, which is divided into four terminals, with Terminals 3 and 4 handling transatlantic flights (British Airways uses Terminal 4). Gatwick is London's second gateway. It has grown from a European airport into an airport that serves 21 scheduled U.S. destinations. A third, new, state-of-the-art airport, **Stansted,** is to the east of the city. It handles mainly European and domestic traffic, although there is a scheduled service from New York. There are fast connections from all the London airports into the capital.

➤ AIRPORT INFORMATION: **Heathrow Airport** (☎ 020/8759–4321). **Gatwick Airport** (☎ 01293/535353). **Stansted Airport** (☎ 01279/680500).

TRANSFERS

From Heathrow: The least expensive route into London is via the **Piccadilly line** of the **Underground** (London's subway system). Trains on the "tube" run every four to eight minutes from all four terminals; the painless 40-minute trip costs £3.40 one-way and connects with London's extensive tube system. The quickest way into London is the new **Heathrow Express** (☎ 0845/600–1515), which ferries travelers in just 15 minutes to and from Paddington Station (in the city center and hub for many of London's Underground city lines). One-way tickets cost £10 for standard class and £20 for first class. Service is daily, from 5:10 AM to 10:40 PM, with departures every 15 minutes.

London Transport (☎ 020/7222–1234) runs two bus services from the airport; each costs £6 one-way and £10 round-trip, and travel time each direction is about one hour. The **Airbus A1** leaves for Victoria Station, with stops along Cromwell Road, at Earls Court, and at Hyde Park Corner every 30 minutes 5:40 AM–8:30 PM. The **Airbus A2** leaves for King's Cross and Euston, with stops at Marble Arch and Russell Square every 30 minutes 6 AM–9:30 PM.

From Gatwick: Fast, nonstop **Gatwick Express** trains leave for Victoria Station every 15 minutes 5:20 AM–12:50 AM, then hourly 1:35 AM–6:05 AM. The 30-minute trip costs £9.50 one-way. A frequent local train also runs all night. Hourly bus services from Gatwick South Terminal Coach Station (5:05 AM–8:20 PM) are provided by **Flightline 777** to Victoria Coach Station. This takes about 90 minutes and costs £7.50 one-way. For details, call Gatwick Traveline (☎ 0990/747777).

From Stansted: London's newest airport, opened in 1991, serves mainly European destinations. The **Stansted Skytrain** to Liverpool Street Station runs every half hour and costs £10.40 one-way, although at press time fares were set to increase.

Cars and taxis drive into London on the M4; the trip can take more than an hour, depending on traffic, from Heathrow. The taxi fare is about £40, plus tip. From Gatwick, the taxi fare is at least £60–£70, plus tip; traffic can be very heavy.

BUS TRAVEL WITHIN LONDON

BUS LINES AND FARES

In central London, buses are traditionally bright red double- and single-deckers, though there are now also many privately owned buses of different colors. Not all buses run the full length of their route at all times; check with the driver or conductor. On some buses you pay the conductor after finding a seat; on others you pay the driver upon boarding. Bus stops are clearly indicated; the main stops have a red LT symbol on a plain white background. When the word "Request" is written across the sign, you must flag the bus down. Buses are a good way of seeing the town, but **don't take one if you are in a hurry.**

Single fares start at 70p for short hops. London is divided into six concentric zones for both bus and tube fares: the more zones you cross, the higher the fare. Regular single-journey or round-trip **One Day Travelcards** (£3.80–£4.50) allow unrestricted travel on bus and tube after 9:30 AM and all day on weekends and national holidays. **LT Cards** (£4.80–£7.50) do not have any restricted times of travel except on N-prefixed Night Buses.

Traveling without a valid ticket makes you liable for an on-the-spot fine (£10 at press time), so always pay your fare before you travel. For more information, there are **LT Travel Information Centres** at the following tube stations: Euston, Hammersmith, King's Cross, Oxford Circus, Piccadilly Circus, St. James's Park, Victoria, and Heathrow (in Terminals 1 and 2); they're open 7:15 AM–10 PM, or call ☎ 020/7222–1234.

NIGHT BUSES

Night buses can prove helpful when traveling in London from 11 PM to 5 AM—these buses add the prefix "N" to their route numbers and don't run as frequently and don't operate on quite as many routes as day buses. You'll probably have to transfer at one of the Night Bus nexuses: Victoria, Westminster, and either Piccadilly Circus or Trafalgar Square. Weekly and monthly Travelcards are good for night buses, but One Day and Weekend Travelcards are not; night bus single fares are also a bit higher than daytime ones. Note: Avoid sitting alone on the top deck of a night bus unless you want to experience the happily rare misfortune of being mugged in London.

DISCOUNT PASSES

Visitor Travelcards (£3.90) available from **BritRail Travel International** are the same as the One Day Travelcards but with the bonus of a booklet of money-off vouchers to major attractions (available only in the United States, for three, four, and seven days).

➤ BUS INFORMATION: **BritRail Travel International** (1500 Broadway, New York, NY 10036, ☎ 212/382–3737).

CAR RENTAL

A car in the city is often more of a liability than an asset. Remember that Britain drives on the left, and the rest of Europe on the right. For more information on navigating the city, *see* Car Travel, *below.*

Rates in London begin at £40 a day and £110 a week for an economy car, usually with manual transmission. Air-conditioning and unlimited mileage generally come with the larger-size automatic car. This does not include 17.5% tax on car rentals.

➤ MAJOR AGENCIES: **Alamo** (☎ 800/522–9696; 020/8759–6200 in the U.K.). **Avis** (☎ 800/331–1084; 800/879–2847 in Canada; 02/9353–9000 in Australia; 09/525–1982 in New Zealand). **Budget** (☎ 800/527–0700; 0144/227–6266 in the U.K.). **Dollar** (☎ 800/800–6000; 020/8897–0811 in the U.K., where it is known as Eurodollar, 02/9223–1444 in Australia). **Hertz** (☎ 800/654–3001; 800/263–0600 in Canada; 020/8897–2072 in the U.K.; 02/9669–2444 in Australia; 03/358–6777 in New Zealand). **National Inter-Rent** (☎ 800/227–3876; 0345/222525 in the U.K., where it is known as Europcar InterRent).

INSURANCE

When driving a rented car you are generally responsible for any damage to or loss of the vehicle. Before you rent see what coverage your personal auto-insurance policy and credit cards already provide.

Collision policies that car-rental companies sell for European rentals usually do not include stolen-vehicle coverage. Before you buy it, check your existing policies—you may already be covered.

REQUIREMENTS & RESTRICTIONS

In London your own driver's license is acceptable (in Great Britain, there is no limit on the age of the driver, but you must be at least 17). An International Driver's Permit is a good idea; it's available from the American or Canadian Automobile Association and, in the United Kingdom, from the Automobile Association or Royal Automobile Club. International permits are universally recognized, and having one may save you a problem with the local authorities.

CAR TRAVEL

The best advice on driving in London is: don't. Because the capital grew up as a series of villages, there never was a central plan for London's streets, and the result is a winding mass of chaos, aggravated by a passion for one-way streets.

EMERGENCIES

➤ CONTACTS: **Automobile Association** (☎ 0990/500600); **Royal Automobile Club** (☎ 0990/722722).

RULES OF THE ROAD

If you must risk life and limb and drive in London, note that the speed limit is 30 mph in the royal parks, as well as in all streets—unless you see the large 40 mph signs (and small repeater signs attached to lampposts) found only in the suburbs. Other basic rules: pedestrians have right-of-way on "zebra" crossings (black and white stripes that stretch across the street between two Belisha beacons—orange-flashing globe lights on posts). The curb on each side of the zebra crossing has zigzag markings. It is illegal to park within the zigzag area or to pass another vehicle at a zebra crossing. At other crossings pedestrians must yield to traffic, but they do have right-of-way over traffic turning left at controlled crossings.

Traffic lights sometimes have arrows directing left or right turns; get into the turn lane if you mean to go straight ahead—don't try to catch a glimpse of the road markings in time. The use of horns is prohibited between 11:30 PM and 7 AM.

THE CHANNEL TUNNEL
Short of flying, the "Chunnel" is the fastest way to cross the English Channel: 35 minutes from Folkestone to Calais, 60 minutes from motorway to motorway, or 3 hours from London's Waterloo Station to Paris's Gare du Nord.

➤ CAR TRANSPORT: **Eurotunnel** (☎ 0990/353–535 in the U.K.).

➤ PASSENGER SERVICE: In the U.K.: **Eurostar** (☎ 0990/186–186), **InterCity Europe** (✉ Victoria Station, London, ☎ 0990/848–848 for credit-card bookings). In the

U.S.: **BritRail Travel** (☎ 800/677–8585), **Rail Europe** (☎ 800/942–4866).

CONSUMER PROTECTION
Whenever shopping or buying travel services in London, **pay with a major credit card** so you can cancel payment or get reimbursed if there's a problem. If you're doing business with a particular company for the first time, **contact your local Better Business Bureau and the attorney general's offices** in your state and the company's home state, as well. Have any complaints been filed? Finally, if you're buying a package or tour, always **consider travel insurance** that includes default coverage (☞ Insurance, *below*).

➤ LOCAL BBBs: **Council of Better Business Bureaus** (✉ 4200 Wilson Blvd., Suite 800, Arlington, VA 22203, ☎ 703/276–0100, FAX 703/525–8277).

CUSTOMS & DUTIES
When shopping, **keep receipts** for all purchases. Upon reentering the country, **be ready to show customs officials what you've bought.** If you feel a duty is incorrect or object to the way your clearance was handled, note the inspector's badge number and ask to see a supervisor. If the problem isn't resolved, write to the appropriate authorities, beginning with the port director at your point of entry.

IN AUSTRALIA

Australia residents who are 18 or older may bring home $A400 worth of souvenirs and gifts (including jewelry), 250 cigarettes or 250 grams of tobacco, and 1,125 ml of alcohol (including wine, beer, and spirits). Residents under 18 may bring back $A200 worth of goods. Prohibited items include meat products. Seeds, plants, and fruits need to be declared upon arrival.

➤ INFORMATION: **Australian Customs Service** (Regional Director, ✉ Box 8, Sydney, NSW 2001, ☎ 02/9213–2000, FAX 02/9213–4000).

IN CANADA

Canadian residents who have been out of Canada for at least seven days may bring home C$500 worth of goods duty-free. If you've been away less than seven days but more than 48 hours, the duty-free allowance drops to C$200; if your trip lasts 24–48 hours, the allowance is C$50. You may not pool allowances with family members. Goods claimed under the C$500 exemption may follow you by mail; those claimed under the lesser exemptions must accompany you. Alcohol and tobacco products may be included in the seven-day and 48-hour exemptions but not in the 24-hour exemption. If you meet the age requirements of the province or territory through which you reenter Canada, you may bring in, duty-free, 1.14 liters (40 imperial ounces) of wine or liquor *or* 24 12-ounce cans or bottles of beer or ale. If you are 16 or older you may bring in, duty-free, 200 cigarettes and 50 cigars. Check ahead of time with Revenue Canada or the Department of Agriculture for policies regarding meat products, seeds, plants, and fruits.

You may send an unlimited number of gifts worth up to C$60 each duty-free to Canada. Label the package UNSOLICITED GIFT—VALUE UNDER $60. Alcohol and tobacco are excluded.

➤ INFORMATION: **Revenue Canada** (✉ 2265 St. Laurent Blvd. S, Ottawa, Ontario K1G 4K3, ☎ 613/993–0534; 800/461–9999 in Canada).

IN NEW ZEALAND

Homeward-bound residents 17 or older may bring back $700 worth of souvenirs and gifts. Your duty-free allowance also includes 4.5 liters of wine or beer; one 1,125-ml bottle of spirits; and either 200 cigarettes, 250 grams of tobacco, 50 cigars, or a combination of the three up to 250 grams. Prohibited items include meat products, seeds, plants, and fruits.

➤ INFORMATION: **New Zealand Customs** (Custom House, ✉ 50 Anzac Ave., Box 29, Auckland, New Zealand, ☎ 09/359–6655, FAX 09/359–6732).

IN THE U.S.

U.S. residents who have been out of the country for at least 48 hours (and who have not used the $400 allowance or any part of it in the past 30 days) may bring home $400 worth of foreign goods duty-free. U.S. residents 21 and older may bring back 1 liter of alcohol duty-free. In addition, regardless of your age, you are allowed 200 cigarettes and 100 non-Cuban cigars. Antiques, which the U.S. Customs Service defines as objects more than 100 years old, enter duty-free, as do original works of art done entirely by hand, including paintings, drawings, and sculptures.

You may also send packages home duty-free: up to $200 worth of goods for personal use, with a limit of one parcel per addressee per day (and no alcohol or tobacco products or perfume worth more than $5); label the package PERSONAL USE and attach a list of its contents and their retail value. Do not label the package UNSOLICITED GIFT or your duty-free exemption will drop to $100. Mailed items do not affect your duty-free allowance on your return.

➤ INFORMATION: **U.S. Customs Service** (inquiries, ✉ 1300 Pennsylvania Ave. NW, Washington, DC 20229, ☎ 202/927–6724; complaints, ✉ Office of Regulations and Rulings, 1300 Pennsylvania Ave. NW, Washington, DC 20229; registration of equip-

ment, ✉ Resource Management, 1300 Pennsylvania Ave. NW, Washington, DC 20229, ☎ 202/927–0540).

ELECTRICITY

To use your U.S.-purchased electric-powered equipment **bring a converter and adapter.** The electrical current in London is 230 volts, 50 cycles alternating current (AC); wall outlets take three-pin plugs, and shaver sockets take two round, oversize prongs.

If your appliances are dual-voltage you'll need only an adapter. Don't use 110-volt outlets, marked FOR SHAVERS ONLY, for high-wattage appliances such as blow-dryers. If you plan to use a laptop, it's a good idea to check with your electrical supplier on the correct type of transformer or adapter you should use.

EMBASSIES

➤ AUSTRALIA: **Australia House** (✉ Strand, WC2, ☎ 020/7379–4334).

➤ CANADA: **MacDonald House** (✉ 1 Grosvenor Sq., W1, ☎ 020/7258–6600).

➤ NEW ZEALAND: **New Zealand House** (✉ 80 Haymarket, SW1, ☎ 020/7930–8422).

➤ UNITED STATES: **U.S. Embassy** (✉ 24 Grosvenor Sq., W1, ☎ 020/7499–9000); for passports, go to the **U.S. Passport Unit** (✉ 55 Upper Brook St., W1, ☎ 020/7499–9000).

EMERGENCIES

➤ DOCTORS & DENTISTS: **Doctor's Call** (☎ 020/8900–1000); **Medical Express,** a private, for-profit outfit (✉ 117A Harley St., W1, ☎ 020/7499–1991); **Eastman Dental Hospital** (✉ 256 Gray's Inn Rd., WC1, ☎ 020/7915–1000) will only administer first aid. **Dental Emergency Care Service** (☎ 020/7955 2186) directs callers to the nearest dental surgery.

➤ EMERGENCY SERVICES: Dial **999** for police, fire, or ambulance.

➤ HOSPITALS: For emergency hospital care, with first treatment free under the National Health Service regulations: **Royal Free Hospital** (✉ Pond St., NW3, ☎ 020/7794–0500) and **University College Hospital** (✉ Grafton Way, WC1, ☎ 020/7387–9300). Most other London hospitals also have emergency rooms.

➤ 24-HOUR PHARMACIES: In Britain, drugstores are called chemists. The leading chain is Boots, but the best bet for hours until midnight is **Bliss the Chemist** (✉ 5 Marble Arch, W1, ☎ 020/7723–6116).

INSURANCE

➤ TRAVEL INSURERS: In the U.S. **Access America** (✉ 6600 W. Broad St., Richmond, VA 23230, ☎ 804/285–3300 or 800/284–8300), **Travel Guard International** (✉ 1145 Clark St., Stevens Point, WI 54481, ☎ 715/345–0505 or 800/826–1300). In Canada **Voyager Insurance** (✉ 44 Peel Center Dr., Brampton, Ontario L6T 4M8, ☎ 905/791–8700; 800/668–4342 in Canada).

➤ INSURANCE INFORMATION: In the U.K. the **Association of British Insurers** (✉ 51–55 Gresham St., London EC2V 7HQ, ☎ 020/7600–3333, FAX 020/7696–8999). In Australia the **Insurance Council of Australia** (☎ 03/9614–1077, FAX 03/9614–7924).

MAIL & SHIPPING

Greater London is divided into 32 boroughs—33, counting the City of London, which has all the powers of a London borough. More useful for finding your way around, however, are the subdivisions of London into various postal districts. Throughout the guide we've listed the full postal code for places you're likely to be contacting by mail, although you'll find the first half of the code more important. The first one or two letters give the location: N means north, NW means northwest, etc. Don't expect the numbering to be logical, however. You won't, for example, find W2 next to W3.

Stamps may be bought from main or subpost offices (the latter are located in stores), from stamp machines outside post offices, and from many newsagents stores and newsstands. Mailboxes are known as post or letter boxes and are painted bright red; large tubular ones are set on the edge of sidewalks, while smaller boxes are set into post-office walls.

POSTAL RATES
Postal rates are as follows: airmail letters up to 10 grams to North America, 43p; postcards, 37p; aerogrammes, 36p. Letters within Britain are 26p for first-class, 20p for second-class. Always check rates in advance, however, as they are subject to change.

MEDIA

NEWSPAPERS & MAGAZINES
For the latest information about shops, restaurants, and art events peruse Britain's glossy monthly magazines—*Tatler, Harpers & Queen, British Vogue, World of Interiors, British House & Garden, The Face,* and *Time Out London.* Many better newsstands around the world also feature the Sunday editions of the leading British newspapers, such as the *London Times,* the *Evening Standard,* the *Independent,* and the *Manchester Guardian;* the "Arts" sections of these papers often have advance news of future events. In addition, these London newspapers have Web sites of their own, full of tips and reviews of the hottest eateries, chicest restaurants, newest hotels.

MONEY MATTERS
A movie in the West End costs £6–£9.50 (at some cinemas less on Monday and at matinees); a theater seat, from £8.50 to about £35, more for hit shows; admission to a museum or gallery, around £5 (though some are free and others request a "voluntary contribution"); coffee, £1–£2; a pint of light (lager) beer in a pub, £2 and more; whiskey, gin, vodka, and so forth, by the glass in a pub, £2.50 and up (the measure is smaller than in the United States); house wine by the glass in a pub or wine bar, around £2, in a restaurant £3.50 or more; a Coke, around 80p; a ham sandwich from a sandwich bar in the West End, £2; a 1-mi taxi ride, £4; an average Underground or bus ride, £1.60, a longer one £2.50.

Prices throughout this guide are given for adults. Substantially reduced fees—generally referred to as "concessions" throughout Great Britain—are almost always available for children, students, and senior citizens. For information on taxes, *see* Taxes, *below.*

ATMS
A credit card or debit card (also known as a check card) will both get you cash advances at ATMs worldwide if your card is properly programmed with your personal identification number. For use in London, your PIN must be four digits long or fewer.

CREDIT CARDS
Throughout this guide, the following abbreviations are used: **AE,**

American Express; DC, Diner's Club; MC, Master Card; and V, Visa.

CURRENCY

The units of currency in Great Britain are the pound sterling (£) and pence (p): £50, £20, £10, and £5 bills; £2, £1 (100p), 50p, 20p, 10p, 5p, 2p, and 1p coins. At press time, the exchange rate was about U.S. $1.65 and Canadian $2.35 to the pound (also known as quid).

CURRENCY EXCHANGES AND BANKS

For the most favorable rates, **change money through banks.** Although ATM transaction fees may be higher abroad than at home, ATM rates are excellent because they are based on wholesale rates offered only by major banks. You won't do as well at exchange booths or bureaux de change in airports or rail and bus stations, in hotels, in restaurants, or in stores—they may advertise attractive exchange rates, but then they can add on hefty commission fees. To avoid lines at airport exchange booths **get a bit of local currency before you leave home.**

London banks are generally open Monday to Friday 9:30 AM to 3:30 PM. Many of the "high street" bank offices remain open until 5 PM, while several of the largest institutions, such as Barclays (208 Kensington High St.), have Saturday hours until noon.

➤ EXCHANGE SERVICES: International Currency Express (☎ 888/842–0880 on East Coast; 888/278–6628 on West Coast). **Thomas Cook Currency Services** (☎ 800/287–7362 for telephone orders and retail locations) has several offices in London, including windows at Victoria Station and Marble Arch (12 Mount St., W1Y,, ☎ 0171/707–8501. **Chequepoint** also has stores throughout London (548 Oxford St., W1, ☎ 0171/723–1005).

TRAVELER'S CHECKS

Lost or stolen checks can usually be replaced within 24 hours. To ensure a speedy refund, buy your own traveler's checks—don't let someone else pay for them: irregularities like this can cause delays. The person who bought the checks should make the call to request a refund.

PACKING

You'll need a heavy coat for winter and a lightweight coat or warm jacket for summer. **Always bring an umbrella and, if possible, a raincoat.** Pack as you would for an American city: jackets and ties for expensive restaurants and nightspots, casual clothes elsewhere. Jeans are popular in London and are perfectly acceptable for sightseeing and informal dining. Blazers and sport jackets are popular here with men. For women, ordinary street dress is acceptable everywhere. If you plan to stay in budget hotels, take your own soap.

PASSPORTS & VISAS

ENTERING GREAT BRITAIN

U.S. and Canadian citizens need only a valid passport to enter Great Britain for stays of up to 90 days. For international travel, **carry a passport even if you don't need one** (it's always the best form of ID), and make **two photocopies of the data page** (one for someone at home and another for you, carried separately from your passport). If you lose your passport, promptly call the nearest embassy or consulate and the local police.

PASSPORT OFFICES

The best time to apply for a passport or to renew is during the fall and winter. Before any trip, check your passport's expiration date, and, if necessary, renew it as soon as possible.

➤ AUSTRALIAN CITIZENS: **Australian Passport Office** (☎ 131–232).

➤ CANADIAN CITIZENS: **Passport Office** (☎ 819/994–3500 or 800/567–6868).

➤ NEW ZEALAND CITIZENS: **New Zealand Passport Office** (☎ 04/494–0700 for information on how to apply; 04/474–8000 or 0800/225–050 in New Zealand for information on applications already submitted).

➤ U.S. CITIZENS: **National Passport Information Center** (☎ 900/225–5674; calls are 35¢ per minute for automated service, $1.05 per minute for operator service).

SIGHTSEEING TOURS

BY BUS

Guided sightseeing tours offer passengers a good introduction to the city from double-decker buses, which are open-topped in summer. Tours run daily and depart (9–5) from Haymarket, Baker Street, Grosvenor Gardens, Marble Arch, and Victoria. You may board or alight at any of about 21 stops to view the sights, and then get back on the next bus. Tickets (£12) may be bought from the driver. These tours include stops at places such as St. Paul's Cathedral and Westminster Abbey. Prices and pickup points vary according to the sights visited, but many pickup points are at major hotels.

➤ TOUR OPERATORS: **Evan Evans** (☎ 020/8332–2222). **Frames Rickards** (☎ 020/7837–3111). **The Original London Sightseeing Tour** (☎ 020/8877–1722). **Big Bus Company** (☎ 020/8944–7810). **Black Taxi Tour of London** (☎ 020/7289–4371).

BY CANAL

In summer, narrow boats and barges cruise London's two canals, the Grand Union and Regent's Canal; most vessels (they seat about 60) operate on the latter, which runs between Little Venice in the west (nearest tube: Warwick Avenue on the Bakerloo Line) and Camden Lock (about 200 yards north of Camden Town tube station). Fares are about £5 for 1½-hour cruises.

➤ CRUISE OPERATORS: **Canal Cruises** (☎ 020/7485–4433). **Jason's Trip** (☎ 020/7286–3428). **London Waterbus Company** (☎ 020/7482–2660).

BY FOOT

One of the best ways to get to know London is on foot, and there are many guided and themed walking tours from which to choose.

➤ TOUR OPERATORS: **Citisights** (☎ 020/8806–4325). **Historical Walks** (☎ 020/8668–4019). **Original London Walks** (☎ 020/7624–3978). Another option is to hire your own Blue Badge accredited guide and tailor your own tour (☎ 020/7495–5504).

BY RIVER

All year round, but more frequently from April to October, boats cruise the Thames, offering a different view of the London skyline. Most leave from Westminster Pier, Charing Cross Pier, and Tower Pier. Downstream routes go to the Tower of London, Greenwich, and the Thames Barrier via Canary Wharf; upstream destinations include Kew, Richmond, and Hampton Court

(mainly in summer). Most of the launches seat between 100 and 250 passengers, have a public-address system, and provide a running commentary on passing points of interest. Depending upon the destination, river trips may last from one to four hours.

➤ RIVER CRUISE OPERATORS: **Catamaran Cruisers** (from Charing Cross to Greenwich; ☎ 020/7839–3572). **Thames Cruises** (☎ 020/7930–3373 for the Thames Barrier and Greenwich). **Westminster Passenger Boat Services** (☎ 020/7930–4097).

A **Sail and Rail** ticket combines the modern wonders of Canary Wharf by Docklands Light Railway with a trip on the river. Tickets are available year-round from Westminster Pier or DLR stations, Canary Wharf, Island Gardens, and Tower Gateway (☎ 020/7363–9700); ticket holders also get discounted tickets to the London Aquarium at Westminster, the Tower Bridge Experience, and the National Maritime Museum, Greenwich.

EXCURSIONS

London Regional Transport, Green Line, Evan Evans, and **Frames Rickards** all offer day excursions by bus to places within easy reach of London, such as Hampton Court, Oxford, Stratford, and Bath.

TAXES

VALUE-ADDED TAX (VAT)

The British sales tax (VAT, Value Added Tax) is 17½%. The tax is almost always included in quoted prices in shops, hotels, and restaurants.

You can **get a VAT refund** by either the Retail Export or the more cumbersome Direct Export method. Many large stores provide these services, but only if you request them; they will handle the paperwork. For the Retail Export method, you must ask the store for Form VAT 407 (you must have identification—passports are best), to be given to customs at your last port of departure. (Lines at major airports can be long, so allow plenty of time.) The refund will be forwarded to you in about eight weeks, minus a small service charge, either in the form of a credit to your charge card or as a British check, which American banks usually charge you to convert. With the Direct Export method, the goods go directly to your home; you must have a Form VAT 407 certified by customs, police, or a notary public when you get home and then sent back to the store, which will refund your money. For inquiries, call the local Customs & Excise office listed in the London telephone directory.

Global Refund is a VAT refund service that makes getting your money back hassle-free. Global Refund services are offered in more than 130,000 shops worldwide. In participating stores, ask for a **Global Refund Cheque** when making a purchase—this Cheque will clearly state the amount of your refund in local currency, with the service charge already incorporated (the service charge equals approximately 3–4% of the purchase price of the item). Global Refund can also process other custom forms, though for a higher fee. When leaving the European Union, get your Global Refund Cheque and any customs forms stamped by the customs official. You can take them to the cash refund office at the airport, where your money will be refunded right there in cash, by check, or a refund to your credit card. Alternatively, you can mail your validated Cheque to Global Refund, and your credit card account will automatically be credited within three billing cyles. Global Refund has a fax-back service further clarifying the process.

➤ VAT REFUNDS: **Global Refund** (✉ 707 Summer St., Stamford, CT 06901, ☎ 800/566–9828).

TAXIS

Those big black taxicabs are as much a part of the London streetscape as the red double-decker buses, yet many have been replaced by the new boxy, sharp-edged model, and the beauty of others is marred by the advertising they carry on their sides. Hotels and main tourist areas have cab stands (just take the first in line), but you can also **flag one down from the roadside.** If the yellow FOR HIRE sign on the top is lit, the taxi is available. Cab drivers often cruise at night with their signs unlit so that they can choose their passengers and avoid those they think might cause trouble. If you see an unlit, passenger-less cab, hail it: you might be lucky.

➤ TAXI FARES: Fares start at £1.40 and increase by units of 20p per 281 yards or 55.5 seconds until the fare exceeds £8.60. After that, it's 20p for each 188 yards or 37 seconds. A 60p surcharge is added on weekday nights 8–midnight and until 8 PM on Saturday. Over Christmas and on New Year's Eve, it rises to £2—and there's 40p extra for each additional passenger. Note that fares are usually raised in April of each year. Tips are extra, usually 10%–15% per ride.

TELEPHONES

COUNTRY & AREA CODES

The country code for Great Britain is 44. Since the summer of 1999, London area codes have been undergoing a major change. In order to facilitate expanded telephone access, British Telecom and other British telephone services are in the process of insti-tuting new codes for all London telephone numbers. The former area codes of 0171 and 0181 are being merged into one London area code—020—with a new pre-fix, either 7 or 8, also being added before the first digit of the old phone number; at press time this procedure was set to begin in June 1999 and run until the official changeover of April 22, 2000. Until that date London numbers can be accessed with parallel sys-tems using *both* forms of area codes; This edition has gone with the 020/7 and 020/8 area coding. Note that the new area codes will effect London's actual telephone numbers—for example, 0171/222–3333 will now become 020/7222–3333, with an increase up to eight digits for the telephone number proper. Under the new system, 0800 numbers and na-tional information numbers of 0345 will not change. Other urban regions (such as Cardiff, Southampton, and Leeds) may also undergo area code changes in the future. Details are on the In-ternet at www.numberchange.org. Within England, there is a help line at 0808/224–2000; from the U.S., additional information and help can be received by dialing 0171/634–8700 (using the old sys-tem) or 020/7634–8700 (using the new system).

When dialing Great Britain from abroad, drop the initial 0 from these local area codes. The coun-try code is 1 for the U.S. and Canada, 61 for Australia, and 64 for New Zealand.

DIRECTORY & OPERATOR INFORMATION

For information anywhere in Britain, dial 192. For the operator, dial 100. For assistance with international calls, dial 155.

INTERNATIONAL CALLS

When calling from overseas to access a London telephone number, drop the 0 from the prefix and dial only 20 (or any other British area code) and then the eight-digit phone number. To give one example: Let's say you're calling Buckingham Palace—020/7839–1377 (or, in the old system, 0171/839–1377)—from the U.S. to inquire about tours and hours. First, dial 011 (the international access code), then 44 (Great Britain's country code), then 20 (London's center city code), then the remainder of the telephone number, 7839–1377, which, under the new area code system, now includes a 7 prefix added to the old number.

LOCAL CALLS

You don't have to dial London's central area code (020) if you are calling inside London itself—just the new eight-digit telephone number.

LONG-DISTANCE CALLS

For long-distance calls within Britain, dial the area code (which begins with 01), followed by the number. The area-code prefix is only used when you are dialing from outside the city. In provincial areas, the dialing codes for nearby towns are often posted in the booth.

LONG-DISTANCE SERVICES

AT&T, MCI, and Sprint access codes make calling long distance relatively convenient, but you may find the local access number blocked in many hotel rooms. First ask the hotel operator to connect you. If the hotel operator balks ask for an international operator, or dial the international operator yourself. One way to improve your odds of getting connected to your long-distance carrier is to travel with more than one company's calling card (a hotel may block Sprint, for example, but not MCI). If all else fails call from a pay phone.

➤ ACCESS CODES: **AT&T Direct** (☎ In the U.K., there are AT&T access numbers to dial the U.S. using three different phone types—Cable & Wireless: 0500/890011; British Telecom: 0800/890011; and AT&T: 0800/0130011; ☎ 800/435–0812 for other areas). **MCI WorldPhone** (☎ In the U.K., dial 0800/890222 for the U.S via MCI; ☎ 800/444–4141 for other areas). **Sprint International Access** (In the U.K., there are Sprint access numbers to dial the U.S. using two different phone types—Cable & Wireless: ☎ 0500/890877; and British Telecom: ☎ 0800/890877; ☎ 800/877–4646 for other areas).

PHONE CARDS

Card phones operate with special cards that you can buy from post offices or newsstands. They are ideal for longer calls; are composed of units of 10p; and come in values of £3, £5, £10, and more. To use a card phone, lift the receiver, insert your card, and dial the number. An indicator panel shows the number of units used. At the end of your call, the card will be returned. Where credit cards are taken, slide the card through, as indicated.

PUBLIC PHONES

There are three types of phones: those that accept (a) only coins, (b) only British Telecom (BT) phone cards, or (c) BT phone cards and credit cards.

The coin-operated phones are of the push-button variety; the workings of coin-operated telephones vary, but there are usually instructions in each unit. Most take 10p, 20p, 50p, and £1 coins. Insert the coins *before* dialing (minimum charge is 10p). If you hear a repeated single tone after dialing, the line is busy; a continual tone means the number is unobtainable (or that you have dialed the wrong—or no—prefix). The indicator panel shows you how much money is left; add more whenever you like. If there is no answer, replace the receiver and your money will be returned.

All calls are charged according to the time of day. Standard rate is weekdays 8 AM–6 PM; cheap rate is weekdays 6 PM–8 AM and all day on weekends, when it's even cheaper. A local call before 6 PM costs 15p for three minutes; this doubles to 30p for the same from a pay phone. A daytime call to the United States will cost 24p a minute on a regular phone (weekends are cheaper), 80p on a pay phone.

TIPPING

Many restaurants and large hotels (particularly those belonging to chains) will automatically add a 10%–15% service charge to your bill, so **always check in advance before you hand out any extra money.** You are, of course, welcome to tip on top of that for exceptional service.

Do not tip movie or theater ushers, elevator operators, or bar staff in pubs—although you may buy them a drink if you're feeling generous. Washroom attendants may display a saucer, in which it's reasonable to leave 20p or so.

Here's a guide for other tipping situations. **Restaurants:** 10%–20% of the check for full meals if service is not already included (when you're paying by credit card, check to see if a service tip has not already been included in the bill before you fill in the correct amount in the total box of your credit slip voucher); a small token if you're just having coffee or tea. **Taxis:** 10%–15%, or perhaps a little more for a short ride.

Porters: 50p–£1 per bag. **Door-men:** £1 for hailing taxis or for carrying bags to check-in desk. **Bellhops:** £1 for carrying bags to rooms, £1 for room service. **Hairdressers:** 10%–15% of the bill, plus £1–£2 for the hair-washer.

UNDERGROUND TUBE TRAVEL

Known colloquially as the "tube," London's extensive Underground system is by far the most widely used form of city transportation. Its easily marked routes, crystal-clear signage, and extensive connections make it a delight to travel. Trains run both beneath and aboveground out into the suburbs, and all stations are clearly marked with the London Underground circular symbol. (In Britain, the word "subway" means "pedestrian underpass.") Trains are all one class; smoking is *not* allowed on board or in the stations.

There are 10 basic lines—all named. The Central, District, Northern, Metropolitan, and Piccadilly lines all have branches, usually taking you to the outlying sections of the city, so **be sure to note which branch is needed for your particular destination.** Electronic platform signs tell you the final stop and route of the next train, and some signs conveniently indicate how many minutes you'll have to wait for the train to arrive. Begun in the Victorian era, the Underground is still being expanded and improved. The East London Line, which runs from Shoreditch and Whitechapel south to New Cross, reopened after major reconstruction in March 1998. As of press time, autumn 1999 was the latest date for the opening of the Jubilee Line extension: when completed, this state-of-the-art subway will sweep from Green Park to London Bridge and Southwark, with connections to Canary Wharf and the Docklands and the much-hyped Millennium Dome, and on to the east at Stratford. At press time, it was touch and go whether visitors would be able to reach the Dome by tube as industrial disputes have hampered and delayed the opening, after which there will be the inevitable teething problems. Optimists still predict the schedule is on track and may open by The Night (although there are rumors to shut the tube network over New Year's Eve, as revelers may well get out of hand). One of the newest lines is the Docklands Light Railway, which runs from Stratford in east London and from Bank and Tower Gateway to Island Gardens. Scheduled for completion in January 2000, the new DLR extension will pass the *Cutty Sark* in Greenwich and then continue on to the razzmatazz of the Millennium Dome (North Greenwich station), terminating at Lewisham.

FARES & SCHEDULES

For both buses and tube fares, London is divided into six concentric zones; the fare goes up the farther out you travel. Ask at Underground ticket counters for the London Transport booklets, which give details of all the various ticket options for the tube. Traveling without a valid ticket makes you liable for an on-the-spot fine (£10 at press time).

For one trip between any two stations, you can buy an ordinary single (one-way ticket) for travel anytime on the day of issue; if you're coming back on the same route the same day, an ordinary return (round-trip ticket) costs twice the single fare. Singles vary in price from £1.40 to £3.40—expensive if you're making several journeys in a day. There are several passes good for both the tube and the bus.

HOURS

Trains begin running just after 5 AM Monday–Saturday; the last services leave central London between midnight and 12:30 AM. On Sunday, trains start two hours later and finish about an hour earlier. Frequency of trains depends on the route and the time of day, but normally you should not have to wait more than 10 minutes in central areas.

PASSES

Several **Travelcards** for tube and bus travel are available at tube and rail stations, as well as some newsstands. These allow unrestricted travel on the tube, most buses, and national railways in the Greater London zones and are valid weekdays after 9:30 AM, weekends, and all public holidays. They cannot be used on airbuses, night buses, or for certain special services. Other options include the following: a **One Day Travelcard** (£3.80–£4.50); **Weekend Travelcards,** for the two days of the weekend and on any two consecutive days during public holidays (£5.70–£6.70); **Family Travelcards,** which are one-day tickets for one or two adults with one to four children (£3–£3.60 with one child, additional children cost 60p each); while the **Carnet** is a book of 10 single tickets valid for central Zone 1 (£10) to use anytime over a year. Up-to-date prices can be found on the LT Web site www.londontransport.co.uk. The **Visitor's Travelcard** may be bought in the United States and Canada for three, four, and seven days' travel; it is the same as the LT Card and has a booklet of discount vouchers to London attractions. In the United States, the Visitor's Travelcard costs $25, $32, and $49, respectively; in Canada, C$29, C$36, and C$55, respectively. Apply to travel agents or, in the United States, to **BritRail Travel International.**

INFORMATION

A pocket map of the tube network is available free from most Underground ticket counters. A large map is on the wall of each platform.

There are LT (London Transport) Travel Information Centres at the following tube stations: Euston, Hammersmith, King's Cross, Liverpool Street, Oxford Circus, Piccadilly Circus, St. James's Park, and Victoria, open 7:15 AM–10 PM; and at Heathrow (in Terminals 1,2 and 4), open 6 AM–3 PM. For information on all London tube and bus times, fares, and so on, dial ☎ 020/7222–1234 (24 hours). For travelers with disabilities, get the free leaflet "Access to the Underground" (☎ 020/ 7918–3312).

➤ UNDERGROUND INFORMATION: **BritRail Travel International** (1500 Broadway, New York, NY 10036, ☎ 212/382–3737).

VISITOR INFORMATION
➤ TOURIST INFORMATION: In the U.S.: **British Tourist Authority** (BTA; ✉ 551 5th Ave., 7th floor, New York, NY 10176, ☎ 212/ 986–2200 or 800/462–2748; 625 N. Michigan Ave., Suite 1510, Chicago, IL 60611 [personal callers only]).

➤ IN CANADA: **British Tourist Authority** (✉ 5915 Airport Rd., Suite 120, Mississauga, Ontario L4V 1T1, ☎ 905/405–1840 or 800/847–4885).

➤ IN THE U.K.: **British Tourist Authority** (✉ Thames Tower, Black's Rd., London W6 9EL, ☎ 020/ 8846–9000).

➤ IN LONDON: Go in person to the **London Tourist Information Centre** at Victoria Station Fore-court for general information (Easter–Oct., daily 8–7; Nov.–Easter, Mon.–Sat. 8–6, Sun. 8:30–4) or to the **British Visitor Centre** (✉ 1 Regent St., Piccadilly Circus SW1Y 4PQ) for travel, hotel, and entertainment information (July–Sept., weekdays 9–6:30, weekends 10–4; May–Sept., weekdays 9–5, Sat. 9–5).

➤ BY PHONE: The London Tourist Board's **VisitorCall** (☎ 0839/ 123456) phone guide to London gives information about events, theater, museums, transport, shopping, and restaurants. A three-month events calendar (☎ 0839/ 123401) and an annual version (☎ 0891/353715) are available by fax (set fax machine to polling mode, or press start/receive after the tone). VisitorCall charges start at 50p per minute, depending on the time of the call. Note that this service is accessible only in the U.K.

WEB SITES
Do check out the World Wide Web when you're planning your trip. You'll find everything from up-to-date weather forecasts to virtual tours of famous cities. Fodor's Web site, **www.fodors.com,** is a great place to start your on-line travels. For more information specifically on London, visit one of the following:

The British Tourist Authority Web site is at **www.visitbritain.com.** Its new "gateway" Web site, www.usagateway.vistibritain.com, focuses on information most helpful to Britain-bound U.S. travelers. The official London web site is www.londontown.com, which also supplies helpful links to other web sites, including Evening Standard Online (www.thisislondon.com); London Transport; The Palace; No. 10 Downing Street; UK Weather; and the BBC (www.bbc.co.uk).

For London events and news months in advance, visit the following culture and entertainment Web sites: www.timeout.co.uk, www.officiallondontheatre.co.uk, and www.ukcalling.co.uk.royal-albert. For the hotel scene in London, visit www.demon.co.uk/hotel-uk. For information about millennium events throughout 2000, click on londonmillenniumcity.com. For the full array of walking tours offered by the excellent Original London Walks, try www.walks.com.

WHEN TO GO

London's weather has always been contrary, and in recent years it has proved red hot and cool by turns. It is virtually impossible to forecast what the pattern might be, but you can be fairly certain that it will not be what you expect. The main feature of British weather is that it is generally mild—with some savage exceptions, especially in summer. Be warned: Air-conditioning is rarely found in places other than department stores, modern restaurants, hotels, and cinemas in London, and in a hot summer you'll swelter. It is also often overcast and damp—though even that has been changing in recent years, with the odd bout of drought. The winter can be rather dismal and is frequently wet and usually cold, but all the theaters, concerts, and exhibitions go full speed. The following list includes the average daily maximum and minimum temperatures for London.

CLIMATE IN LONDON

➤ FORECASTS: **Weather Channel Connection** (☎ 900/932–8437), 95¢ per minute from a Touch-Tone phone.

LONDON

Jan.	43F	6C	May	62F	17C	Sept.	65F	19C
	36	2		47	8		52	11
Feb.	44F	7C	June	69F	20C	Oct.	58F	14C
	36	2		53	12		46	8
Mar.	50F	10C	July	71F	22C	Nov.	50F	10C
	38	3		56	14		42	5
Apr.	56F	13C	Aug.	71F	21C	Dec.	45F	7C
	42	6		56	13	38	4	

1 Destination: London

THE CITY OF VILLAGES

LONDON IS AN enormous city—600 square mi—on a tiny island, hosting about 7 million Londoners, ⅛ of the entire population of England, Scotland, and Wales; but it has never felt big to me. It is fashioned on a different scale from other capital cities, as if, given the English penchant for modesty and understatement, it felt embarrassed by its size. Each of the 32 boroughs that comprise the whole has its own attitude, and most are subdivided into yet smaller enclaves exhibiting yet more particular behaviors, so that there is really no such person as a generic Londoner. Stay here long enough, and Professor Higgins's feat of deducing Eliza Dolittle's very street of birth from the shape of her vowels will seem like nothing special. It's a cliché, but London really is a city of villages.

I have lived in several of these, and I am fluent in the language of a few others, but my village, Holland Park, is the one I know best, and it illustrates as well as any how London is changing. Holland Park is small—just a few streets surrounding the former grounds of Holland House, a Jacobean mansion whose remains (it was bombed during World War

II) now house a restaurant, a gallery, an open-air theater, and a youth hostel. North of the park, Holland Park Avenue metamorphoses into the windy local high street, Notting Hill Gate, then into bleak Bayswater Road, abutted on its right by Kensington Gardens and Hyde Park, before breaking, where the main London gallows once stood, into irritating, commercial Oxford Street. But here, for a few West Eleven moments (postal-district terminology you'd do well to master to help with navigation), it is a broad, plane tree–lined boulevard strung with vast white-stucco late-Victorian houses and looking an awful lot like Paris.

In our sophisticated age, the European ambience of Holland Park Avenue has been seized upon by niche marketers, and we now have two French patisseries, three international newsstands, a BMW showroom, and a candlelighted Provençal restaurant within a couple of blocks. The history racket is doing similar things all over town, history being what London has to sell now that it no longer cuts much ice in the world economy. It would be sentimental to prefer the avenue's old hardware store and late-night family grocer (open till 9!) to the fancy

Continental shops that have replaced them—London's got to move with the times, after all.

Both good and bad come with the new territory. The Pakistani family who used to take turns minding the grocery store bought the block a decade later. Those Patels are now a well-known London dynasty, with most of the capital's newsstands in their empire—a satisfying reversal of roles from the British Raj days. Meanwhile, homeless Londoners (the number is about 100,000, and rising) work the overpriced yuppie supermarket threshold selling their magazine, *The Big Issue,* for a profit of 25p per guilty conscience. As one of the many villages built during Victoria's reign, Holland Park is a neighborhood unaccustomed to urban blight. But much of London has weathered several centuries of coping with the indigent population.

That's one of the best things about the city: everything has been seen before, and history is forever poking its nose in. Whatever you're doing, you're doing it on top of a past layered like striated rock. You can see the cross sections clearly sometimes, as in the City, where lumps of Roman wall nest in the postmodern blocks of the street helpfully named London Wall. Walk toward the Thames to Cheapside, which you can tell was the medieval marketplace if you know the meaning of "ceap" ("to

barter"), and there's the little Norman church of St. Mary-le-Bow, rebuilt by Wren and then again after the Blitz, but still ringing the Bow Bells. Then look to your right, and you'll be gobsmacked by the dome of St. Paul's. Of course, all you really wanted was to find a place for lunch—nearly impossible on a weekend in this office wasteland.

Instead of going weak-kneed at the sights, Londoners are apt to complain about such privations while pretending simultaneously that no other city in the United Kingdom exists. Edinburghers and Liverpudlians can complain till Big Ben tolls 13, but Londoners continue to pull rank with a complacency that amuses and infuriates visitors in about equal measure. London definitely *used* to be important. The vein of water running through its center has always linked the city with the sea, and it once gave British mariners a head start in the race to mine the world's riches and bring them home. The river proved convenient for building not only palaces (at Westminster, Whitehall, Hampton Court, Richmond, Greenwich) but an empire, too.

The empire dissolved, but the first Thames bridge is still there, in almost the same spot that the emperor Claudius picked in AD 43, and although the current drab concrete incarnation dates only from 1972, it's still called London

Bridge. The Tudor one was much better—something I learned before I was 10 from visits to the Museum of London, which used to be in nearby Kensington Palace. I liked the old bridge because of the row of decapitated heads stuck on poles above the gatehouse, which you could see on the model. It added a frisson to history, which more recent exhibitions, like the amazingly popular London Dungeon, have rather cynically packaged.

The old London Bridge lasted 600 years. Lined with shops and houses, it presided over a string of fairs *on* the Thames, when winters were colder and the water froze thick. Nowadays we rarely see a snowfall, though we'll talk endlessly about its possibility. We are genuinely obsessed by the weather because we have so much of it, though most of it is damp. Snow varies the scenery, stops any tube train with an overground route, makes kids of everyone with a makeshift toboggan and access to a park (99% of the population), and fosters a community spirit normally proscribed by the city's geography and its citizens' cool. Winters were colder as recently as the '60s, when waiting for the crust to thicken enough to skate on the Round Pond in Kensington Gardens—now good only for model-boat sailors and duck feeders—was only a matter of time.

The corollary to our temperate winter, though, is a fresh confidence in summer sufficient to support herds of sidewalk tables. Holland Park Avenue no longer has the monopoly on Parisian ambience. All over town, an epidemic of Continental-style café chains serving croissants and *salade frisée* has devoured the traditional tobacco-stained pubs serving warm bitter and bags of pork scratchings. Most of the remaining pubs have turned into faux-Edwardian parlors with coffee machines and etchings or, more recently, wood-floored bars serving flavored vodkas and Tuscan food. The change has been going on for about a decade, and it suits London, as does its momentous discovery that restaurants are allowed to serve good food in smart surroundings and not charge the earth.

London is increasingly a European city, as if England were no longer stranded alone in the sea. In fact, ever since airplanes superseded ships, this island race has been undergoing an identity crisis, which reached its apogee in the '70s when Prime Minister Edward Heath sailed us irrevocably into the Common Market. Occasionally Britain still holds out against some European Community legislation or other, attempting to reassert differences that are following executions at the Tower and British Colonial supremacy into history. But however much the social climate changes, London is built on a firm foundation. Until the ravens desert the Tower of London—which is when, they say, the kingdom will fall—we have Westminster Abbey and St. Paul's and the Houses of Parliament, the Georgian squares and grand Victorian houses, the green miles of parks, the river, the museums and galleries and theaters, and 32 boroughs of villages to keep us going.

–Kate Sekules

NEW & NOTEWORTHY

From the vantage point of mid-1999—a.k.a. the precursor to the big 2000—England is poised on toe-points in its rush to embrace the turning of the century. The question is: is everything ready? The epicenter of the celebrations, the awesome Millennium Dome in Greenwich, is due to open on December 31, 1999, although the new lines of Underground Tube transport to and from the Millennium Borough may not be up and running by then, due to months of industrial turbulence and setbacks. Londoners will probably resort to that time-honored mode of transport called old Father Thames and take the ferry from the new streamlined Charing Cross Pier, now called Embankment Pier. This is another new landmark which has been the brainchild of the "new" Labour party, propelled by the prime minister, Tony Blair. His energetic enthusiasm is reflected in the exciting projects unveiled by some of London's most venerable museums. Every museum, in fact, is in a whirlwind of activity. Classicism spearheaded by innovation is the byword: for the glittering new Great Court of the British Museum; the latest technological gizmos at the staid British Library; the state-of-the-art new branch of the Tate Gallery now installed at the futuristic Bankside Power Station; the multimillion-pound makeovers of the Sadlers Wells Theatre and the Royal Opera House; the new face of the National Portrait Gallery; and the scintillating space-age Earth Galleries at the Science Museum. Thanks to these attractions, swinging-again London now outranks its neighbors as Europe's most future forward spot.

The Greenwich Millennium Dome, a multimillion-pound 320-m structure designed by architect-provocateur Richard Rogers, is terribly controversial; whether this is a must-see or an expensive mistake is not possible to say at press time, but it is certainly the most costly monument to the advent of the new millennium. Over two and a half miles in circumference with a roof a mile high, it is also very large indeed. If you head out to the Millennium Borough of Greenwich before the Dome opens, you can drop in on the Millennium Experience Visitor Centre (Pepys House, Royal Naval College), with its graphic displays, models, videos, and interactive monitors designed for the locals. May 2000 will see the 10-day Millennium Maritime Festival in the vicinity, with 2,000 vessels moored in and around Docklands. Other major building projects in London include the new Tate Gallery of Modern Art, being installed in the former Bankside Power Station. Culturally, London is making a bid to catch up with its overseas rivals in terms of modern art and the word here is that big is beautiful—opening in May 2000, the new Tate will house the huge number of works of art formerly hidden from public view due to lack of space in the old Millbank Gallery. Also going up on the south side of the Thames is the British Airways London Eye—the world's tallest Ferris wheel. Famed architect Sir Christopher Wren, architect of St. Paul's Cathedral, probably wouldn't be too delighted by this amusement park ride soaring over central London—or would he?

Among London's other attractions, check out the new British Library, which already offers selected services to researchers. The less academic can revel in its public-friendly offerings: the Italianate piazza-style entrance, the touch-screen access to subjects ranging from the Magna Carta to mega rock stars, and the glass edifice which houses King George's library. Kensington Palace has reopened its renovated Royal Dress Collection. The National Portrait Gallery is no longer the poor, cramped neighbor of the big National Gallery. The end of 1998 saw the rats banished from the basement, which was transformed into a bright new café and bookshop. The staid bastion of the British Museum is putting on a bold new face on the subject of the ownership of the Elgin Marbles. These controversial treasures are now shown in a grand, modern setting and their history brought up-to-date with a tactile, interactive display in the Parthenon Galleries. The Natural History Museum is perfecting its biggest project since it opened in 1881, the Earth Galleries, which examine earthly phenomena, like volcanoes, tornadoes, and deserts, and then take you out into space and onto other planets. While at Westminster Abbey, the earth is positively moving, as a recent visitor discovered when the floor gave way beneath him and brought him too close to the corpses of ancient history for comfort. Too many old bones crumbling beneath, and the weight of too many tourists have weakened the floor in areas; if remedial work is carried out, disruption will be minimal. Finally, polished and ready to meet the world after four years' restorative work, the Albert Memorial in Kensington Gardens was revealed in all its newly gilded glory in late 1998. Like the Albert Memorial, all of London is putting on a bold new face worthy of the momentum of the new millennium.

PLEASURES AND PASTIMES

The Performing Arts

There isn't *a* single London "arts scene"—there is an infinite variety of them. As long as there are audiences for Feydeau revivals, drag queens, obscure teenage rock bands, hit musicals, body-painted dancers, and improvised stand-up comedy, someone will figure out how to stage them. Admission prices are not always bargain-basement, but when you consider the cost of a London hotel room, the city's arts and entertainment are easily affordable.

To find out what's showing during your stay, the weekly magazine *Time Out* (it comes out every Wednesday; Tuesday in central London) is an invaluable resource. The *Evening Standard*—especially the Thursday edition—also carries listings, as do the "quality" Sunday papers and the Saturday *Independent, Guardian,* and *Times.* You'll find racks overflowing with leaflets and flyers in most cinema and theater foyers,

and you can pick up the free bi-monthly "London Theatre Guide" leaflet from most hotels as well as from tourist information centers.

Music

London is home to four world-class orchestras. The London Symphony Orchestra is in residence at the Barbican Centre, while the London Philharmonic lives at the Royal Festival Hall—one of the finest concert halls in Europe. Between the Barbican and South Bank, there are concert performances almost every night of the year. The Barbican also presents chamber-music concerts in partnership with such celebrated orchestras as the City of London Sinfonia. The Royal Albert Hall during the Promenade Concert season—July through September—is an unmissable pleasure. Also look for the lunchtime concerts held throughout the city in either smaller concert halls, arts-center foyers, or churches; they usually cost less than £5 or are free. St. John's, Smith Square, and St. Martin-in-the-Fields are the major venues and also present evening concerts.

Theater

From Shakespeare to the umpteenth year of *Les Misérables* (or "The Glums," as it's affectionately known), London's West End has the cream of the city's theater offerings. But there's much more to see in London than the offerings of Theatreland and the national companies: of the 100 or so legitimate theaters operating in the capital, only about half are officially "West End," while the remainder fall under the blanket title of "Fringe," which encompasses everything from off-the-wall "physical theater" to premieres of new plays and revivals of old ones.

Shakespeare, of course, supplies the backbone to the theatrical life of the city. There can hardly have been a day since the one on which the Bard breathed his last, when one of his plays, in some shape or form, was not being performed. On the London stage, they have survived being turned into musicals (from Purcell to rock); they have made the reputations of generations of famous actors (and broken not a few); they have seen women playing Hamlet and men playing Rosalind. If the Bard of Bards remains the headliner at Stratford-upon-Barbican, the London theater scene is amazingly varied. From a West End *Oliver* revival to an East End feminist staging of *Ben-Hur,* London remains a theatergoer's town.

Opera and Ballet

For decades, London's leading troupes, the Royal Opera and the Royal Ballet, have shared grandiose quarters at the Royal Opera House in Covent Garden—a fact that rather cut down on the number of opera and ballet performances that could be mounted

in a season. Even with a backstage renovation done several years ago, there was still a great pressure on rehearsal and dressing room space. Now change is finally here: the grand Opera House is reopening in December 1999 after a major two-year renovation, with quite literally—as anyone who has sat through a performance on a hot, humid night will testify—enough breathing space for public and performers.

The Delights of Dining

London now ranks among the world's top dining scenes. A new generation of chefs has precipitated a fresh approach to food preparation, which you could call "London-style" though most refer to it as "Modern British." Everyone seems to have an opinion about it, and newspapers and magazines devote pages to food and restaurant reviews. Everyone reads them and everyone dines out to the point where London has become the most significant foodies' town in Europe. The days are long gone when British cuisine was best known for shepherd's pie—ubiquitously available in pubs (though not made according to the song from *Sweeney Todd,* "with real shepherd in it")—and fish-and-chips. As it turns out, there is a new return to British favorites, with old standbys like bangers and mash getting the nouvelle treatments with such modish garnishes as sausages of wild boar and potato purée with pesto. It probably won't be long before some of-the-moment hot spot unveils a trendy variation on the nursery-rhyme pie, with four-and-twenty rock stars popping out in place of blackbirds to sing for the king. This thriving dining scene rests on a solid foundation of ethnic cuisines. Thousands of (mostly northern) Indian restaurants have long ensured that Londoners view access to a tasty tandoori as a birthright. Chinese—Cantonese, primarily—restaurants in London's tiny Chinatown and beyond have been around a long time, as have Greek tavernas, and there are even more Italian restaurants than Indian. Now add Thai, Malaysian, Spanish, and Japanese cuisines to those easily found in England's capital. After all this, traditional British food, lately revived from a certain death, appears as one more exotic cuisine in the pantheon. If, in fact, you're out for traditional English food, but with a stylish twist, head to London's hot new "gastro-pubs."

The Pub Experience

Londoners could no more live without their "local" than they could forgo dinner. The pub—or public house, to give it its full title—is ingrained in the British psyche as social center, refuge, second home. Pub culture—revolving around pints, pool, darts, and sports—is still male-dominated; however, as a result of the gentrification trend that was launched in the late '80s by the major breweries (which own most pubs), transforming many ancient smoke- and spittle-stained dives into fantasy Edwardian drawing rooms, women have been entering their welcoming doors in increasing numbers. This decade, the trend has been toward the Bar, identified by its cocktail list, creative paintwork, bare floorboards, and chrome fittings, and to the "gastro-pub," where a good kitchen fuels the relaxed ambience. These are English pubs, but not as we formerly knew them. When doing a London pub crawl, you must remember one thing: arcane licensing laws forbid the serving of alcohol after 11 PM (10:30 on Sunday; there are different rules for restaurants)—a circumstance you see in action at 10 minutes to 11, when the "last orders" bell triggers a stampede to the bar.

QUICK TOURS

In a city with as many richly stocked museums and marvels as London, visitors risk seeing half of everything and all of nothing. If you're here for just a short period you need to plan carefully so you don't miss the must-see sights. The following itineraries will help you structure your visit efficiently. See the neighborhood exploring tours in Chapter 2 for more information about individual sights.

Tour One

Think London 101, as this tour encompasses sights that have played a central role in British history. Start your day at postcard-London, the **Houses of Parliament,** best viewed from Westminster Bridge and the Statue of Boudicca. If you're lucky, you'll hear Big Ben chiming as you head across Parliament Square to breathtakingly beautiful **Westminster Abbey.** Commune with Chaucer's spirit at the abbey's Poets' Corner, then head back past Parliament to the boulevard called Whitehall. On the left side is **10 Downing Street,** home to Tony Blair, the charismatic Prime Minister. Farther up on the right side is the 17th-century **Banqueting House;** inside are grand Rubens paintings, outside, King Charles II was beheaded in 1649. Continue north past **Horse Guards Parade**—a perfect photo-op with two splendid mounted guards on duty—to Trafalgar Square and **Nelson's Column.** Head to the **National Gallery** for a flip-book-fast tour of some of the world's greatest paintings. After lunch at the museum's Brasserie, head directly east to the beloved 18th-century **St. Martin-in-the-Fields** church, with its soaring spire and London Brass-Rubbing Centre. For your finale, pass under elegant Admiralty Arch on the southwest corner of Trafalgar Square to take in a grand view of **Buckingham Palace** at the end of The Mall.

Tour Two

A right royal gathering of sights make up the itinerary for this tour, which takes in Buckingham Palace, the aristocratic St. James's district, and some regal streets. Begin in the morning at Piccadilly Circus and head west along Piccadilly to browse at No. 181, which is Fortnum and Mason, the exclusive department store that supplies the Queen's groceries; a block south is Jermyn Street, address to some of London's ritziest gentlemen's shops and Floris, at No. 89, where royalty since Queen Victoria have selected their favorite perfumes. From here, head south on Duke of York Street to drink in pedigree-proud St. James's Square, then head west along King Street to St. James's Place and **Spencer House,** built by Princess Diana's 18th-century ancestors (tours are given on Sunday only). Continuing south along St. James's Street you can pay a call on Prince Charles—or rather, take a look at his St. James's Palace; if you're a fan of his grandmother, walk southwest along Cleveland Row, then turn left onto Stable Yard Row to see the Queen Mum's Clarence House. Continue south on Marlborough Street to The Mall, designed in 1911 as a grand promenade to **Buckingham**

Palace. Arrive at the palace gates in time for the 11:30 Changing of the Guard (daily April–July; alternate days August–March). If the palace is open for public tours (generally August through early October), take in Her Majesty's digs; if not, take a hoof along Constitution Hill to Hyde Park Corner and feast your eyes for at least an hour on the sumptuous salons of "No. 1 London"—**Apsley House,** the Duke of Wellington's mansion. You should be ravenous for lunch by now, so hop on the nearby Hyde Park Corner tube to Green Park and return to Fortnum & Mason for afternoon tea upstairs or to The Fountain (closed Sunday).

Tour Three

London-at-its-most-spectacular is served up on this tour, which includes St. Paul's Cathedral, the Tower of London, and Shakespeare's Globe, plus some Cinerama-size views of London along the Thames. Get a jump on the crowds by tubing it to Tower Hill and being at the **Tower of London** when the gates open. After marveling at the Crown Jewels, ponder the end of Anne Boleyn and give your regards to the Tower ravens. Then tube it over to nearby **St. Paul's Cathedral**—London's symbolic heart and scene of Princess Diana's wedding. Head aloft to the cathedral's Whispering Gallery and Christopher Wren's dome for some great views, then return to earth and the 17th-century neighborhood called Blackfriars, southwest of St. Paul's. Wander through the picturesque alleys and courtyards down to the Thames and Blackfriars Bridge. Fuel up with some pub grub at London's most amazing pub, the Black Friar, across from the Black-Friars tube station, then head out over the bridge to Southwark. Take a left turn to stroll down the beautiful river esplanade to **Shakespeare's Globe Theatre** and, a stone's throw away, Christopher Wren's own house, built on Cardinal's Cap Alley so he could watch the construction of his cathedral across the river. Relax by the banks of Father Thames.

Tour Four

Literary and legal London are the highlights here, as we wind our way from the fabled British Museum to Covent Garden. From the Russell Square tube, pass Bloomsbury Square—once haunt of Virginia Woolf, E. M. Forster, and Lytton Strachey—to Mankind's Attic, a.k.a. the **British Museum.** After a whirlwind tour of its legendary treasures, head east to **Dickens House.** To the southwest lies **Lincoln's Inn** and Lincoln's Inn Fields, address to **Sir John Soane's Museum,** a stately, dotty delight that is home to one of London's most extraordinary collections of art, antiques, and bric-a-brac.

Time for lunch and charming Covent Garden beckons. Erstwhile home to Eliza Doolittle, the **Covent Garden Piazza** is now home to outdoor cafés and cosmopolitan shops.

FODOR'S CHOICE

No two people will agree on what makes a perfect vacation, but it's fun and helpful to know what others think. Here's a compendium drawn from the must-see lists of hundreds of tourists. We hope you'll have a chance to experience some of these great memories-in-the-making yourself while visiting London. For detailed information about entries, refer to the appropriate chapters within this guidebook.

Long Live the Queen!

★ **Changing of the Guard.** Adding a dash of color to the gloomiest of London days, this ceremony is mounted (daily, depending on the season) at both Whitehall and Buckingham Palace.

★ **The Mall.** Look down this grand thoroughfare to Buckingham Palace from underneath Admiralty Arch and you'll see what the Queen sees during all those royal ceremonies.

★ **Trooping the Colour.** Marking the Queen's birthday in June (the

real one is in April), this is the capital's most spectacular military occasion, with bands playing, flags fluttering, and massed ranks of soldiers in scarlet coats and immense "busbies."

Quintessential London

★ **The Houses of Parliament at sunset.** Cross the Thames to Jubilee Gardens to see this view of London at its storybook best.

★ **Sunday Afternoon at Speakers' Corner, Hyde Park.** A space especially reserved for anyone with anything to say that they *must* say publicly makes for great entertainment. Speakers seem to be most oratorical on Sunday afternoons.

★ **St. Paul's Cathedral Thameside.** The most thrilling vantage point to take in St. Paul's is at Cardinal Cap's Alley, across the Thames on the southern embankment, right by Shakespeare's Globe Theatre.

★ **An Afternoon Performance at Shakespeare's Globe Theatre.** This new, spectacular, open-to-the-skies reconstruction of Shakespeare's beloved "wooden O" magically transports you back to Elizabethan London. In 16th-century fashion, audience participation is welcome: jump in and hiss Iago—you'll have plenty of company.

★ **Tower Bridge at Night.** A dramatically floodlighted Tower

Bridge confronts you as you come out of the Design Museum on a winter's night.

Fascinating Walks

★ **Beatles' Magical Mystery Tour.** This wonderful stroll down Memory Lane offered by Original London Walks includes the London Palladium, No. 3 Savile Row—the Fab Four's London headquarters—and Abbey Road.

★ **A Belgravia Promenade.** Far from the madding crowd, Belgravia represents all that is gracious in London living. A vision out of a Regency-period engraving, Belgrave Place is one of the most moneyed addresses in town and adorned with elegant mansions and picturesque mews.

★ **Jack the Ripper Walk.** Several organizations offer tours of "Jack's London"—the East End and its grisly settings for the Whitechapel murders. Unforgettable!

London Splendor

★ **Apsley House.** Known as No. 1 London, this was the august residence of the Duke of Wellington, fabled conqueror of Napoléon. The house's centerpiece, the Waterloo Gallery, is one of the grandest rooms in Europe.

★ **Linley Sambourne House.** A little masterpiece of Victoriana, this former residence of *Punch* cartoonist Linley Sambourne is unusually charming.

★ **Sir John Soane's Museum.** Eccentric architect of the Bank of England, Sir John left his house to the nation on condition nothing be changed; the result is a phantasmagoria of colors, unusual perspectives, and artifacts from many centuries.

★ **Spencer House.** The London house to end all London houses, this glamorous 18th-century Palladian pile was built by Princess Diana's ancestors. Now restored to all its glory by Lord Rothschild, it proves the 18th-century Spencers were no slouches in the flash department.

★ **Wallace Collection.** The serene 18th-century mansion, Hertford House, that shelters this sumptuous collection, is as much a part of the appeal as its rich array of porcelain, paintings, furniture, and sculptures.

Magnificent Museums

★ **British Museum.** You could move into this grand pile and never tire of all that it has to offer, from the Rosetta Stone to the Mildenhall Treasure. Best of all are the beautiful Elgin Marbles from ancient Greece.

★ **Tate Gallery.** The greatest glories of English painting are here, from Elizabethan portraits to the most avant avant-garde works.

★ **National Gallery.** Da Vincis, Rubenses, and Rembrandts fill the rooms here—an incomparably rich treasure trove of Old Masters.

Comforts

★ **Claridge's.** The same fine qualities that attracted the King of Morocco, among many others, to this world-renowned Mayfair hotel are sure to make you feel right at home, too. ££££

★ **Covent Garden Hotel.** Discerning travelers now call this the most stylish hotel in London. ££££

★ **The Dorchester.** It's a true accomplishment that so much gold leaf and marble, linens and brocades have managed the effect of sophisticated intimacy in this hotel that has all of Hyde Park as its front garden. ££££

★ **The Savoy.** Secure a river suite at this historic, late-Victorian hotel overlooking the Thames, and you'll get one of the best stays—and views—in London. ££££

★ **Beaufort.** It's fair to use this set of Victorian houses, run by a wonderfully friendly all-female staff, as a home away from home, especially if you live practically next door at Harrods. £££

★ **The Pelham.** Designed to capture the essence of English country housedom, Tim and Kit Kemp's boutique hotel offers the comforting feel of a tranquil country retreat with all the advantages of being in the center of South Kensington. £££

★ **The Commodore.** Secreted in a quiet square behind Bayswater Road, this family-run hotel has some great value duplex-style rooms. ££

★ **The Vicarage.** Friendly and homey, this Kensington B&B has kept high standards for years. £

Flavors

★ **La Tante Claire.** Pierre Kaufman may be London's best chef. The decor is light and sophisticated, the service impeccable, the French wine list impressive, but the food is the point. Walk your meal off afterward along the nearby Thames embankment. ££££

★ **Oak Room.** Marco Pierre White enjoys Jagger-like fame as he ventures where few chefs have gone before. His kitchen is dizzyingly creative: be prepared for grand style—foie gras, caviar, and truffles—done with a truly adventurous hand. The room—a Belle-Epoque extravaganza—is one of London's most beautiful. ££££

★ **Le Caprice.** This glamorous place has stood the test of time—the food is great, the ambience even better. The other reason everyone comes here is that everyone else does, which leads to the best people-watching in town. £££

★ **Quaglino's.** This isn't the biggest, but it is still the best of Sir Terence Conran's London hot spots. Now past its fifth birthday, "Quags" is *the* out-of-towners' post-theater or celebration destination, while Londoners like its late hours. £££

★ **Rules.** Come, escape from the 20th century. London's answer to Maxim's in Paris, this enjoys an incomparably beautiful setting, one that has welcomed everyone from Dickens to the Duke of Windsor. The food is good but the decor is truly delicious. £££

★ **Zafferano.** London's best Italian restaurant has attracted Princess Margaret, Eric Clapton, Joan Collins, and any number of snazzy neighborhood Belgravians. The decor is ho-hum, but try pumpkin ravioli with a splash of amaretto. £££

★ **Maison Novelli.** Jean Christophe Novelli is one of the new cult heroes of mod Brit cuisine, and foodies flock to up-and-coming Islington to check out his Rabelaisian dishes. ££–£££

★ **The American Bar.** This dazzling bar at the Stafford Hotel, covered with college ties, toys, and antique U.S. memorabilia, is one of London's most delightful interiors. ££

★ **The Cow.** Notting Hillbillies and other stylish folk adore this luxe "gastro-pub." A serious chef whips up Tuscan/British specialties but some diners prefer the half-dozen Irish rock oysters with a pint of Guinness. ££

★ **Wódka.** Laid back and stylish, this serves London's only modern Polish food. Order from the separate menu a carafe of the purest vodka in London (and watch the check inflate). ££

★ **The Black Friar.** The ornate building with a statue of a friar on the front near Blackfriars tube station is one of London's most splendiferous pubs—all colored marble, inlaid mother-of-pearl, and stained glass. The pub grub is minimal, but the pints and the fetching locals are great. £

★ **George Inn.** London at its time-machine best, this inn sits in a courtyard where Shakespeare's plays were performed. The building dates from the 17th century, and it is London's last remaining galleried inn. £

2 Exploring London

LONDON GREW FROM A WOODEN BRIDGE built over the Thames in the year AD 43 to its current 600 square mi and 7 million souls in haphazard fashion, meandering from its two official centers: Westminster, seat of government and royalty, and the City, site of finance and commerce. However, London's *un*official centers multiply and mutate year after year, and it would be a shame to stop only at the postcard views. Life is not lived in monuments, as the patrician patrons of the great Georgian architects understood when they commissioned the city's elegant squares and town houses. Close by, Westminster Abbey's original vegetable patch (or convent garden), which became the site of London's first square, Covent Garden, is now an unmissable stop on any agenda.

If the great, green parks are, as in Lord Chatham's phrase, "the lungs of London," then the River Thames is its backbone. The South Bank section absorbs the Southwark stews of Shakespeare's day and the current reconstruction of his original Globe Theatre, the concert hall from the '50s Festival of Britain, the arts complex from the '70s, and—farther downstream—the gorgeous 17th- and 18th-century symmetry of Greenwich, where the world's time is measured.

White Card Museum Pass

If museums are at the top of your sightseeing list, the White Card offers free admission into 15 major museums for a basic card fee. The museums are Apsley House; Barbican Art Gallery; Courtauld Gallery at Somerset House; Design Museum; Hayward Gallery; Imperial War Museum; London Transport Museum; Museum of London; Museum of the Moving Image; National Maritime Museum/Old Royal Observatory/Queen's House, Greenwich; Natural History Museum; Royal Academy of Arts; Science Museum; Theatre Museum; and Victoria and Albert Museum. The basic fee is 16 pounds, adult ticket, for 3 days; also available are family tickets and adult tickets for 7 days. The White Card is available at any of the museums listed above, or call ☎ 020/7923–0807.

Central London Exploring *(Boxes Refer to Detail Maps)*

Regent's Park

Regents Park Area

Abbey Rd.
Abercorn Pl.
Holt Rd.
Clifton Rd.
Bloomfield Rd.
Harrow Rd.
Wellington Rd.
Grove End Rd.
Circus Rd.
St. John's Wood Rd.
Prince Albert Rd.
Canal Circus
Park Rd.
Inner Circle
Chester Rd.
Outer Circle
Albany St.
Hampstead Rd.
Eversholt St.

Euston Station

Bloomsbury Legal

Euston Rd.
Gower St.
Tottenham Court Rd.

Marylebone Rd.
Praed Street
Edgware Rd.
Gloucester Pl.
Baker St.
Bond St.
Portland Pl.
Harley St.
Wigmore St.

Soho and Covent Garden

Oxford

Regent St.
Charing Cross

Piccadilly Circus

Paddington Station

Sussex Gdns.

Bayswater Rd.

Hyde Park

Park Lane

Sth. Audley St.

Piccadilly

Green Park

Constitution Hill

Pall Mall

The Mall

St. James's Park

Birdcage Walk

Kensington Gardens

W. Carriage Dr.

The Serpentine

Kensington Gore

Kensington Rd.

S. Carriage Rd.

Knightsbridge

Brompton Rd.

Sloane St.

Pont St.

Belgrave Square

Eaton Square

Wilton Rd.

Victoria St.

Horseferry

Victoria Station

Horse

Westminster and Royal London

Kensington, Knightsbridge, Mayfair, Belgravia and Hyde Park

Cromwell Rd.

Sloane Ave.

Sloane Sq.

King's Rd.

Royal Hospital Rd.

Pimlico Rd.

Lupus St.

Grosvenor

Rd.

Fulham Rd.
Sydney St.
Old Church St.
Oakley St.
Cheyne Walk
Chelsea Embankment
Chelsea Br. Rd.
Chelsea Br.

River Thames

Nine Elms Ln.

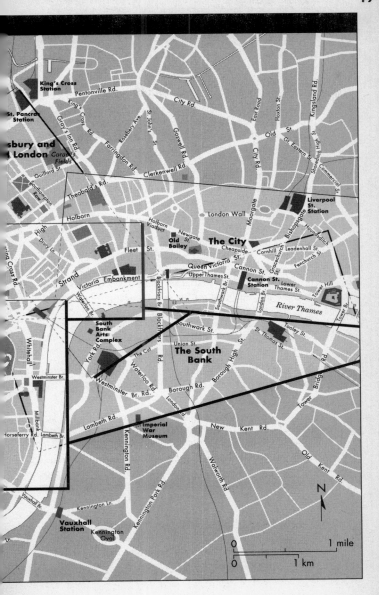

King's Cross
Station

St. Pancras
Station

Pentonville Rd.

City Rd.

sbury and
l London

*Coram's
Fields*

Guilford St.

Southampton
Row

Theobald's Rd.

Clerkenwell Rd.

Holborn

London Wall

Moorgate

Liverpool
St.
Station

Bishopsgate

Houndditch

King's Cross Rd.

Gray's Inn Rd.

Farringdon Rd.

Goswell Rd.

City Rd.

Rosebury Ave.

St. John's St.

Old St.

Gt. Eastern St.

Shoreditch High St.

Commercial St.

Kingsland Rd.

Hoxton St.

East Road

High Holborn

Drury La.

Holborn
Viaduct

Newgate
St.

Old
Bailey

The City

Cheapside

Cornhill

Leadenhall St.

Gracechurch St.

Fenchurch St.

Tower Hill

Charing Cross Rd.

Fleet St.

Victoria Embankment

Strand

Queen Victoria

Cannon St.

Upper Thames St.

Blackfriars Br.

Cannon St.
Station

Lower
Thames St.

London Br.

Southwark Br.

Tower Br.

River Thames

Whitehall

South
Bank
Arts
Complex

York Rd.

Blackfriars Rd.

The Cut

Southwark St.

Union St.

St. Thomas St.

Tooley St.

The South
Bank

Waterloo Br.

Westminster Br.

Westminster Br. Rd.

Waterloo Rd.

Borough Rd.

Borough High St.

London Rd.

Tower Bridge Rd.

Millbank

Horseferry Rd.

Lambeth Br.

Lambeth Rd.

Kennington Rd.

Imperial
War
Museum

New

Kent Rd.

Walworth Rd.

Old Kent Rd.

Kennington Park Rd.

Vauxhall Br.

Kennington Ln.

Vauxhall
Station

Kennington
Oval

N

0		1 mile

0		1 km

Westminster and Royal London

Westminster and Royal London might be called "London for Beginners." If you went no farther than these few acres, you would have seen many of the famous sights, from the Houses of Parliament, Big Ben, Westminster Abbey, and Buckingham Palace, to two of the world's greatest art collections, housed in the National and Tate galleries. You can truly call this area Royal London, since it is neatly bounded by the triangle of streets that make up the route that the Queen usually takes when journeying from Buckingham Palace to Westminster Abbey or to the Houses of Parliament on state occasions. The three points on this royal triangle are Trafalgar Square, Westminster, and Buckingham Palace. Naturally, in an area that regularly sees the pomp and pageantry of royal occasions, the streets are wide and the vistas long. With beautifully kept St. James's Park at the heart of the triangle, there is a feeling here of timeless dignity—flower beds bursting with color, long avenues of ancient trees framing classically proportioned buildings, constant glimpses of pinnacles and towers over the treetops, the distant *bong!* of Big Ben counting off the hours. This is concentrated sightseeing, so pace yourself. Remember that for a large part of the year, much of Royal London is floodlighted at night, adding to the theatricality of the experience.

Numbers in the text correspond to numbers in the margin and on the Westminster and Royal London map.

Sights to See

⑩ Banqueting House. Commissioned by James I, Inigo Jones (1573–1652), one of England's great architects, created this banqueting hall in 1619–1622 out of an old remnant of the Tudor Palace of Whitehall. Influenced by Andrea Palladio's work, which he saw during a sojourn in Italy, Jones remade the palace with Palladian sophistication and purity. James I's son, Charles I, enhanced the interior by employing the Flemish painter Peter Paul Rubens to glorify his father all over the ceiling. As it turned out, these allegorical paintings, depicting a wise monarch being received into heaven, were the last thing Charles saw before he was beheaded on a scaffold outside in 1649. ⊠ *Whitehall,* ☎ *020/7930–4179.* ◱ *£3.60.* ☼ *Mon.–Sat. 10–5. Tube: Westminster.*

Westminster and Royal London

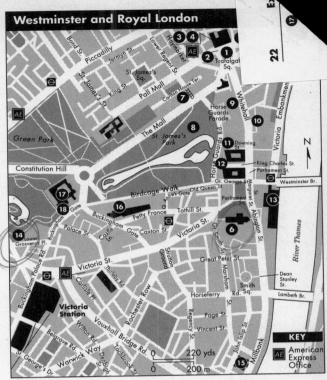

Banqueting House, **10**

Buckingham Palace, **17**

Cabinet War Rooms, **12**

Carlton House Terrace, **7**

Horse Guards Parade, **9**

Houses of Parliament, **13**

National Gallery, **3**

National Portrait Gallery, **4**

Nelson's Column, **2**

Queen's Gallery, **18**

Royal Mews, **14**

St. James's Park, **8**

St. Martin-in-the-Fields, **5**

Tate Gallery, **15**

Ten Downing Street, **11**

Trafalgar Square, **1**

Wellington Barracks, **16**

Westminster Abbey, **6**

Buckingham Palace. Supreme among the symbols of London, indeed of Britain generally, and of the Royal Family, Buckingham Palace tops the must-see lists—although the building itself is no masterpiece and has housed the monarch only since Victoria moved here from Kensington Palace on her accession in 1837. Its great gray bulk sums up the imperious splendor of so much of the city: stately, magnificent, and ponderous. In 1824 the palace was substantially rebuilt by John Nash, that tireless architect, for George IV, that tireless spendthrift. Compared to other great London residences, it is a Johnny-come-lately affair: the Portland stone facade dates from only 1913, and the interior was renovated and redecorated only after World War II bombs damaged it. It contains some 600 rooms, including the State Ballroom and, of course, the Throne Room. These State Rooms are where much of the business of royalty is played out—investitures, state banquets, receptions, lunch parties for the famous, and so on. The royal apartments are in the north wing; when the Queen is in, the royal standard flies at the masthead. The State Rooms are on show for eight weeks in August and September, when the royal family is away. The **Changing of the Guard,** which, with all the pomp and ceremony monarchists and children adore, remains one of London's best free shows; it culminates in front of the palace. Marching to live music, the Queen's Guard proceeds up the Mall from St. James's Palace to Buckingham Palace. Shortly afterward, the new guard approaches from Wellington Barracks via Birdcage Walk. Once the old and new guards are in the forecourt, the gold guard symbolically hands over the keys to the palace. The ceremony takes place daily at 11:30 AM April–July, and on alternating days August–March, but the guards sometimes cancel due to bad weather; check the signs in the forecourt or call 089/150–5452. Arrive by 10:30 AM for a decent view of all the panoply. ✉ *Buckingham Palace Rd., SW1,* ☎ *020/7839–1377, 020/7799–2331 for 24-hour information, 020/7321–2233 credit-card reservation line (AE, MC, V), subject to a 50p booking charge.* 🎫 *£10.* ☉ *Early Aug.–early Oct. (confirm dates, which are subject to Queen's mandate), daily 9:30–4:15. Tube: St. James's Park, Victoria.*

⑫ Cabinet War Rooms. It was from this small maze of 17 bomb-proof underground rooms—in back of the hulking Foreign Office—that Britain's World War II fortunes were directed. During air raids, the Cabinet met here—the Cabinet Room is still arranged as if a meeting were about to convene; in the Map Room, the Allied campaign is charted; the Prime Minister's Room holds the desk from which Churchill made his morale-boosting broadcasts; and the Telephone Room has his hotline to FDR. ✉ *Clive Steps, King Charles St.,* ☎ *020/7930–6961.* 🎫 *£4.80.* 🕐 *Daily 10–5:15. Tube: Westminster.*

❼ Carlton House Terrace. A glorious example of Regency architect John Nash's genius, Carlton House Terrace was built between 1812 and 1830, under the patronage of George IV (Prince Regent until George III's death in 1820). Nash was responsible for a seies of West End developments, of which these white-stucco facades and massive Corinthian columns may be the most imposing. Today, the structure houses the **Institute of Contemporary Art,** better known as the ICA, one of Britain's leading modern-art centers. The ICAfé offers good hot dishes, salads, quiches, and desserts. The bar upstairs, which serves baguette sandwiches, has a picture window overlooking the Mall. ✉ *The Mall,* ☎ *020/7930–3647.* 🎫 *1-day membership £1.50, additional charge for specific events.* 🕐 *Daily noon–9:30, later for some events. Tube: Charing Cross.*

❾ Horse Guards Parade. Facing Horse Guards Road—opposite St. James's Park at one end and Whitehall at the other—Horse Guards Parade is now notable mainly for the annual Trooping the Colour ceremony, in which the Queen takes the Royal Salute, her official birthday gift, on the second Saturday in June. (Like Paddington Bear, the Queen has two birthdays; her real one is on April 21.) There is pageantry galore, with marching bands and the occasional guardsman fainting clean away in his weighty busby (those curious, furry hats). Covering the vast expanse of the square that faces Horse Guards Road, opposite St. James's Park, at one end, and Whitehall at the other, the ceremony is televised and also broadcast on Radio 4. You can also see it from the Mall, but you have to get there very early in the morning for any kind of decent view. You can also attend the queenless rehearsals on the preceding two Saturdays. At the Whitehall facade of Horse Guards, two mounted sentries known as the Queen's Life Guard provide what may be London's most frequently exercised photo op, held every morning. ⊙ *Whitehall Life Guard ceremony: Mon.–Sat. 11 am, Sun. 10 am.*

★ ⓭ **Houses of Parliament.** Seat of Great Britain's government, the Houses of Parliament are, arguably, the city's most famous and photogenic sight. Facing them you see, from left to right: Big Ben—keeping watch on the corner, the Houses of Parliament themselves, Westminster Hall (the oldest part of the complex), and the Victoria Tower. The most romantic view of the complex is from the opposite, south, side of the river, a vista especially dramatic at night when the spires, pinnacles, and towers of the great building are floodlighted green and gold. After a catastrophic fire in 1834, these buildings arose, designed in a delightful mock-medieval style by two Victorian-era architects: Sir Charles Barry and Augustus Pugin. The Palace of Westminster, as the complex is still properly called, was established by Edward the Confessor in the 11th century. It has served as the seat of English administrative power, on and off, ever since.

Now virtually the symbol of London, the 1858 **Clock Tower** designed by Pugin contains the bell known as Big Ben that chimes the hour (and the quarters); weighing a mighty 13 tons, the bell takes its name from Sir Benjamin Hall, the far-from-slim Westminster building works commissioner. At the other end of Parliament is the 336-ft-high **Victoria Tower,** newly agleam from its recent restoration and cleaning. The rest of the complex was scrubbed down some years ago; the revelation of the honey stone under the dowdy, smog-blackened facades, which seemed almost symbolic at the time, cheered London up no end. There are two Houses, the Lords and the Commons. The Visitors' Galleries of the House of Commons affords a view of the best free show in London, staged in the world's most renowned ego chamber (if you want to take it in during its liveliest hour, Prime Minister's Question Time, you'll need to book tickets in advance). The private residence of the Lord Chancellor within the Palace of Westminster has recently reopened after a spectacular renovation; be sure to have your name

Hilton

> Portobello Road

placed in advance on the waiting list for the twice-weekly tours—press coverage of the refurbishment has generated great demand. Note that lines for the House of Commons are always long, so try to come early. ⊠ *St. Stephen's Entrance, St. Margaret St., SW1,* ☎ *020/7219–3000; 020/ 7219–4272 (Commons information); 020/7219–3107 (Lords information); 020/7219–2394 (Lord Chancellor's Residence).* 🎟 *Free.* ☉ *Commons Mon.–Thurs. 2:30–10, Fri. 9:30–3 (although not every Fri.); Lords Mon.–Thurs. 2:30–10; Lord Chancellor's Residence Tues. and Thurs. Tube: Westminster.*

★ ❸ **National Gallery.** Jan Van Eyck's *Arnolfini Marriage,* Leonardo da Vinci's *Virgin and Child,* Velázquez's *Rokeby Venus,* Constable's *Hay Wain . . .* you get the picture. There are approximately 2,200 other paintings in this museum—many of them instantly recognizable and among the most treasured works of art anywhere. The museum's low, gray, colonnaded, neoclassic facade fills the north side of Trafalgar Square. The collection ranges from painters of the Italian Renaissance and earlier—housed in the 1991 Sainsbury Wing, designed by the American architect Robert Venturi—through the Flemish and Dutch masters, the Spanish school, and of course the English tradition, including Hogarth, Gainsborough, Stubbs, and Constable.

The collection is really too overwhelming to absorb in a single viewing. The **Micro Gallery,** a computer information center in the Sainsbury Wing, might be the place to start. You can access in-depth information on any work here, choose your favorites, and print out a free personal tour map that marks the paintings you most want to see. Rounding out the top-10 list (the first four lead off above) are Uccello's *Battle of San Romano* (children love its knights on horseback), Bellini's *Doge Leonardo Loredan* (notice the snail-shell buttons), Botticelli's *Venus and Mars,* Caravaggio's *Supper at Emmaus* (almost cinematically lit), Turner's *Fighting Téméraire* (one of the artist's greatest sunsets), and Seurat's *Bathers at Asnières.* Note that free admission encourages repeat visits: although you may plan to see just the top of the top, the National Gallery, like so many first-rate collections, reveals more gems the more one explores. A major exhibition on works from Renaissance Florence heralds in the millennium. For a great time-out and fashionable lunch, head for the museum's Brasserie, in the Sainsbury Wing. ⊠ *Trafalgar Sq., WC2,* ☎ *020/7747–2885 (information).* ⊠ *Free; charge for special exhibitions.* ⊙ *Mon.–Sat. 10–6, Sun. 10–6; June–Aug., Wed. until 9; 1-hr guided tour starts at Sainsbury Wing weekdays at 11:30 and 2:30, Sat. 2 and 3:30. Tube: Charing Cross.*

★ ❹ **National Portrait Gallery.** Just around the corner from the National Gallery, this is a much more idiosyncratic collection that presents a brief history of Britain through its people, past and present; it is an essential visit for all history and literature buffs. As an art collection it is eccentric, since the subject, not the artist, is the point. Highlights range from Holbein to Hockney. Many of the faces are obscure and will be just as unknown to English visitors, because the portraits outlasted their sitters' fame—not so surprising when the portraitists are such greats as Reynolds, Gainsborough, Lawrence, and Romney. But the annotation is comprehensive, the layout is easy to negotiate, being chronological, with the oldest at the top—and there is a new, separate research center for those who get hooked on particular personages. Don't miss the new Victorian and early 20th-century portrait galleries. ⊠ *St. Martin's Pl.,* ☎ *020/7306–0055.* ⊠ *Free.* ⊙ *Weekdays 10–5, Sat. 10–6, Sun. 2–6. Tube: Charing Cross, Leicester Sq.*

❷ **Nelson's Column.** Centerpiece of Trafalgar Square, this famed landmark is topped with E. H. Baily's 1843 statue of Admiral Lord Horatio Nelson, keeping watch from his 145-ft-high granite perch. The bas-reliefs depicting scenes of his life, installed around the base, were cast from cannons he captured. The four majestic lions, designed by the Victorian painter Sir Edwin Landseer, were added in 1867. The calling cards of generations of picturesque pigeons have been a corrosive problem for the statue; this may have been finally solved by the addition of a gel coating to the statue.

⓲ **Queen's Gallery.** Housed in a former chapel at the south side of **Buckingham Palace,** this showcase offers a rotating sample of what is generally regarded as the finest private art collection in the world. The most famous pictures, including Vermeer's *The Music Lesson* and works by Rubens, Rembrandt, and Canaletto are usually on view in Buckingham Palace or the State Apartments at Windsor Castle. Smaller, often themed, selections from the vast holdings are presented here. On October 10, 1999, however, the gallery is closing for a complete renovation and will not reopen until 2002. ⊠ *Buckingham Palace Rd., SW1,* ☎ *020/7799–2331.* ▣ *£4, combined ticket for Queen's Gallery and Royal Mews £6.70.* ☉ *Tues.–Sat. 9:30–4:30, Sun. 2–4:30. Closed for renovation Oct. 10, 1999–2002. Tube: St. James's Park, Victoria.*

☝ ⑭ **Royal Mews.** Unmissable children's entertainment, this museum is the home of Her Majesty's Coronation Coach. Standing nearly next door to the Queen's Gallery, the Royal Mews were designed by famed Regency-era architect John Nash. Mews were originally falcons' quarters (the name comes from their "mewing," or feather-shedding), but horses gradually eclipsed birds of prey. Now some of the magnificent royal beasts live here alongside the fabulous, bejeweled, glass and golden coaches they draw on state occasions. ⊠ *Buckingham Palace Rd., SW1,* ☎ *020/7839–1377.* ▣ *£3.70, combined ticket for Queen's Gallery and Royal Mews £6.70.* ☉ *Aug. 2–Sept. 30, Mon.–Thurs. 10:30–4:30; Oct. 1–Aug. 1 Mon.–Thurs. 12–4. Closed Mar. 25–29, Dec. 23–Jan. 5. Tube: St. James's Park, Victoria.*

❽ **St. James's Park.** London's smallest, most ornamental park and the oldest of its royal ones, St. James's Park makes a spectacular frame for the towers of Westminster and Victoria—especially at night, when the illuminated fountains play and the skyline beyond the trees looks like a floating fairyland. Its present shape more or less reflects what John Nash designed under George IV, turning the canal into a graceful lake (which was cemented in at a depth of 4 ft in 1855, so don't even think of swimming) and generally naturalizing the gardens. More than 30 species of birds—including swans that belong to the Queen—congregate on Duck Island at the east end of the lake. Along the northern side of the park, you'll find the grand thoroughfare known as **The Mall**—best seen on those days when the Queen is hosting her garden parties and it is thronged with hundreds of guests on their way to Buckingham Palace, most of whom have donned hat and frock to take afternoon tea with the monarch. At dusk on summer days, the deck chairs (which you must pay to use) are often crammed with office lunchers being serenaded by music from the bandstands. But the best time to stroll the leafy walkways is after dark, with Westminster Abbey and the Houses of Parliament rising above the floodlighted lake, and peace reigning.

⑤ St. Martin-in-the-Fields. One of Britain's best-loved churches, St. Martin's was completed in 1726; James Gibbs's classi-cal-temple-with-spire design became a familiar pattern followed for churches in early Colonial America. The church is also a haven for music lovers, since the internationally known Academy of St. Martin-in-the-Fields was founded here, and a popular program of free lunchtime and evening concerts continues today. The church's fusty interior has a wonderful atmosphere for music making—but the wooden benches can make it hard to give your undivided attention to the music. The **London Brass-Rubbing Centre**, where you can make your own souvenir knight from replica tomb brasses, with metallic waxes, paper, and instructions provided, is in the crypt. ⊠ *Trafalgar Sq.*, ☎ *020/7930–0089; 020/7839–8362 credit-card bookings for evening concerts.* 🎫 *Brass rubbings from £1.* ☉ *Church daily 8–8, crypt Mon.–Sat. 10–8, Sun. noon–6. Tube: Charing Cross, Leicester Sq.*

⑮ Tate Gallery. The Tate—everyone drops the word "gallery"— overlooks the Thames, about a 20-minute walk from the Houses of Parliament, and is widely known as Britain's leading collection of modern art. "Modern" is slightly misleading, since one of the three collections here consists of British art from 1545 to the present, including works by Hogarth, Gainsborough, Reynolds, and Stubbs from the 18th century, and by Constable, Blake, and the Pre-Raphaelite painters from the 19th. Also from the 19th century is the J. M. W. Turner Bequest, now housed magnificently in the James Stirling–designed **Clore Gallery**, the largest collection of work by this leading British romantic artist. The Tate has an innovative policy of rehanging the whole gallery annually, which means that a favorite work may not be on view. Usually, however, your tour can deal you multiple pleasing shocks of recognition (Rodin's *The Kiss*, Lichtenstein's *Whaam!*). ✉ *Millbank, SW1,* ☏ *020/7821–1313 or 020/ 7821–7128.* 🎫 *Free; special exhibitions £3–£7.* ☉ *Daily 10–5:50. Tube: Pimlico.*

⓫ **Ten Downing Street.** South of the Banqueting House (☞ *above*), you'll find the British version of the White House, occupying three unassuming 18th-century houses. No. 10 has been the official residence of the prime minister since 1732. The cabinet office, hub of the British system of government, is on the ground floor; the prime minister's private apartment is on the top floor. The chancellor of the exchequer occupies No. 11. Downing Street is cordoned off, but you should be able to catch a glimpse of it from Whitehall. *Tube: Westminster.*

❶ **Trafalgar Square.** Permanently alive with people, Londoners and tourists alike, and roaring traffic, Trafalgar Square remains London's "living room"—great events, such as royal weddings, elections, sporting triumphs—will always see the crowds gathering in the city's most famous square. It is a commanding open space—originally built to reflect the width and breadth of an empire that once reached to the farthest corners of the globe—containing a bevy of must-see attractions, including **Nelson's Column** (☞ *above*) and the **National Gallery** (☞ *above*). Today, street performers enhance the square's intermittent atmosphere of celebration, which is strongest in December, first when the lights on the gigantic Christmas tree are turned on, and then—less festively—when thousands gather to see in the New Year.

⓰ **Wellington Barracks.** This is the august headquarters of the Guards Division, the Queen's five regiments of elite foot guards who protect the sovereign and patrol her palace dressed in tunics of gold-purled scarlet and tall busbies of Canadian brown bearskin. If you want to learn more about the guards, you can visit the **Guards Museum;** the entrance is next to the Guards Chapel. ✉ *Wellington Barracks, Birdcage Walk,* ☏ *020/7930–4466 or ext. 3430.* 🎫 *£2.* ☉ *Sat.–Thurs. 10–4. Tube: St. James's Park.*

★ ❻ **Westminster Abbey.** Nearly all of Britain's monarchs have
been crowned here since the coronation of William the
Conqueror on Christmas Day 1066—and most are buried
here, too. The main nave is packed with atmosphere and
memories, as it has witnessed many splendid coronation ceremonies, royal weddings, and more recently, the funeral of
Diana, Princess of Wales. It is also packed with crowds, so
much so these days that in March 1998 an admission
charge (a steep one, at that) was set in place for entrance
to the main nave. Other than the mysterious gloom of the
vast interior, the first thing that strikes most people is the
fantastic proliferation of statues, tombs, and commemorative
tablets: in parts, the building seems more like a stonema-
son's yard than a place of worship. But it is in its latter capacity that this landmark truly comes into its own. Although
attending a service is not something to undertake purely
for sightseeing reasons, it provides a glimpse of the abbey
in its full majesty, accompanied by music from the Westminster choristers and the organ that Henry Purcell once
played.

The present abbey is a largely 13th- and 14th-century rebuilding of the 11th-century church founded by Edward
the Confessor, with one notable addition being the 18th-
century twin towers over the west entrance, completed by
Sir Christopher Wren. The nave is your first sight on entering; you need to look up to gain a perspective on the truly
awe-inspiring scale of the church, since the eye-level view
is obscured by the choir screen, past which point admission is charged. Before paying, look at the poignant **Tomb
of the Unknown Warrior,** an anonymous World War I mar-
tyr who lies buried here in memory of the soldiers fallen in
both world wars. Passing through the Choir, with its mid-
19th-century choir stalls, into the North Transept, look up
to your right to see the painted-glass Rose Window, the
largest of its kind. You can then proceed into one of the
architectural glories of Britain, the **Henry VII Chapel,** passing the huge white marble tomb of Elizabeth I, buried with
her half-sister, "Bloody" Mary I. All around are magnificent sculptures of saints, philosophers, and kings, with
wild mermaids and monsters carved on the choir-stall mis-
ericords (undersides), and exquisite fan vaulting above

(binoculars will help you spot the statues high on the walls)—the last riot of medieval design in England and one of the miracles of Western architecture.

Next you enter the **Chapel of Edward the Confessor,** where beside the royal saint's shrine stands the **Coronation Chair,** which has been briefly graced by nearly every royal posterior. In 1400 Geoffrey Chaucer became the first poet to be buried in **Poets' Corner,** which also has memorials devoted to William Shakespeare, William Blake, and Charles Dickens. Exit the abbey by a door from the South Transept. Outside the west front is an archway into the quiet, green **Dean's Yard** and the entrance to the **Cloisters** and the **Brass-Rubbing Centre** (☎ 020/7222–2085). ⊠ *Broad Sanctuary, SW1,* ☎ *020/7222–5152.* ✉ *£5; Undercroft, Pyx Chamber, Chapter House, and Treasury, £2.50 (1£ if you bought ticket to abbey).* ☉ *Mon.—Sat. 9–3:45; last admissions Sat. 1:45. Undercroft, Pyx Chamber, Chapter House, and Treasury Apr.–Oct., daily 10:30–5:30; Nov.–Mar., daily 10:30–4. Closed weekdays to visitors during services. Tube: Westminster.*

Soho and Covent Garden

A quadrilateral bounded by Regent Street, Coventry/Cranbourn streets, Charing Cross Road, and the eastern half of Oxford Street encloses Soho, the most fun part of the West End. This appellation, unlike the New York neighborhood's similar one, is not an abbreviation of anything, but a blast from the past—derived (as far as we know) from the shouts of "So-ho!" that royal huntsmen in Whitehall Palace's parklands were once heard to cry. One of Charles II's illegitimate sons, the Duke of Monmouth, was an early resident, his dubious pedigree setting the tone for the future: for many years Soho was London's strip show/peep show/clip joint/sex shop/brothel center. The mid-'80s brought legislation that granted expensive licenses to a few such establishments and closed down the rest. Today, Soho remains the address for many wonderful ethnic restaurants, including those of London's Chinatown.

Best known as Eliza Doolittle's stomping grounds in Shaw's *Pygmalion* and Lerner and Loewe's *My Fair Lady,* the

32

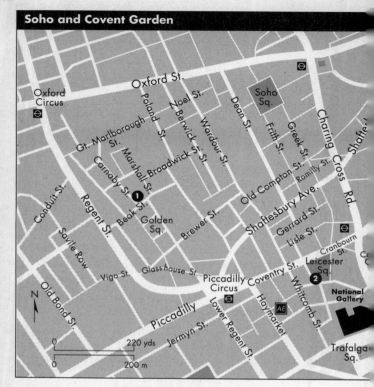

Soho and Covent Garden

Oxford Circus
Oxford St.
Poland St.
Noel St.
Berwick St.
Wardour St.
Dean St.
Soho Sq.
Frith St.
Greek St.
Charing Cross Rd.
Shaftes...
Gt. Marlborough St.
Carnaby St.
Marshall St.
Broadwick St.
Old Compton St.
Romilly St.
Conduit St.
Regent St.
Beak St.
Golden Sq.
Brewer St.
Shaftesbury Ave.
Gerrard St.
Lisle St.
Savile Row
Cranbourn St.
Leicester Sq.
National Gallery
Vigo St.
Glasshouse St.
Piccadilly Circus
Coventry St.
Whitcomb St.
Old Bond St.
Piccadilly
Lower Regent St.
Haymarket
Trafalga Sq.
Jermyn St.

N

0   220 yds
0   200 m

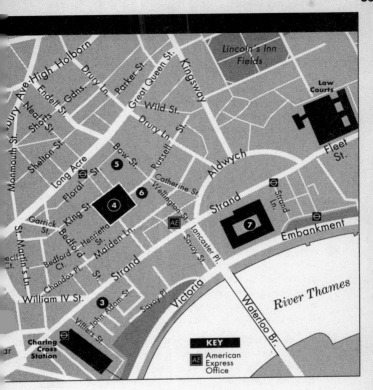

Lincoln's Inn Fields

Law Courts

Monmouth St.

...bury Ave.·High Holborn

Drury Ln.

Endell St.

Shorts Gdns.

Parker St.

Great Queen St.

Neal St.

Kingsway

Shelton St.

Wild St.

Drury Ln.

St.

Long Acre

Bow St.

5

Floral St.

Russell St.

Catherine St.

Wellington St.

Aldwych

Strand

Strand Ln.

Garrick St.

King St.

4

6

Bedford

Henrietta St.

St.

Ct.

Bedford Ct.

Maiden Ln.

AE

Lancaster Pl.

Savoy St.

7

Embankment

Chandos Pl.

Cecil Ct.

St. Martin's Ln.

Strand

Savoy Pl.

Victoria

Waterloo Br.

River Thames

William IV St.

3

John Adam St.

Villiers St.

Fleet St.

Charing Cross Station

KEY

AE American Express Office

former Covent Garden Market became the Piazza in 1980, and it still functions as the center of a neighborhood—one that has always been alluded to as "colorful." It was originally the "convent garden" belonging to the Abbey of St. Peter at Westminster (later Westminster Abbey). Centuries of magnificence and misery, vice and mayhem, and more recent periods of art-literary bohemia followed, until it became the vegetable supplier of London when its market building went up in the 1830s, followed by the Flower Market in 1870. When the produce moved out to the bigger, better Nine Elms Market in Vauxhall in 1974, the (now sadly defunct) Greater London Council stepped in with a rehabilitation scheme, and a new neighborhood was born.

Numbers in the text correspond to numbers in the margin and on the Soho and Covent Garden map.

Sights to See

❸ Adelphi. Near the triangular-handkerchief Victoria Embankment Gardens, this regal riverfront row of houses was the work of all four of the brothers Adam (John, Robert, James, and William: hence the name, from the Greek *adelphoi,* meaning "brothers"), London's Scottish architects. The best mansion is 7 Adam Street.

❶ Carnaby Street. The '60s synonym for swinging London fell into a post-party depression, reemerging sometime during the '80s as the main drag of a public-relations invention called West Soho. Blank stares would greet anyone asking directions to such a place, but it is geographically logical, and the tangle of streets—Foubert's Place, Broadwick Street, Marshall Street—do cohere, at least, in type of merchandise (youth accessories, mostly, with a smattering of designer boutiques).

❼ Courtauld Institute Galleries. Several years ago, this collection was moved to a setting worthy of its fame: a grand 18th-century classical mansion, Somerset House. Founded in 1931 by the textile maven Samuel Courtauld, this is London's finest Impressionist and Post-Impressionist collection (Manet's *Bar at the Folies-Bergère* is the star), with bonus Baroque works thrown in. ✉ *The Strand,* ☎ *020/7873–2526.* ◩ *£4; White Card accepted.* ⊙ *Mon.–Sat. 10–6, Sun. noon–6. Tube: Temple, Embankment.*

❹ Covent Garden (The Piazza). The original "convent garden" produced fruits and vegetables for the 13th-century Abbey of St. Peter at Westminster. In 1630, the Duke of Bedford, having become owner, commissioned Inigo Jones to lay out a square, with St. Paul's Church at one end. The fruit, flower, and vegetable market established in the 1700s flourished until 1974, when its traffic grew to be too much for the narrow streets, and it was moved south of the Thames. Since then, the area has been transformed into the Piazza, a mostly higher-class shopping mall, which features a couple of cafés and some knickknack stores that are good for gifts. Open-air entertainers perform under the portico of St. Paul's Church, where George Bernard Shaw set the first scene of *Pygmalion* (reshaped as the musical *My Fair Lady*).

❷ Leicester Square. This is the big magnet for nightlife lovers. Looking at the neon of the major movie houses, the fast-food outlets, and the disco entrances, you'd never guess the square—it's pronounced "lester"—was laid out around 1630. The Odeon, on the east side, is the venue for all the Royal Film Performances, and the movie theme is continued by a jaunty little statue of Charlie Chaplin in the opposite corner. Shakespeare sulks in the middle, chin on hand, clearly wishing he were somewhere else. One landmark certainly worth visiting is the **Society of London Theatre (SOLT) ticket kiosk**, on the southwest corner, which sells half-price tickets for many of that evening's performances (☞ Nightlife and the Arts, *below*).

❺ Royal Opera House. The fabled home of the Royal Ballet and Britain's finest opera company is set to open in December 1999, when mammoth renovations will try to bring this 19th-century treasure into the 21st. Here, in days of yore, Joan Sutherland brought down the house as Lucia di Lammermoor, and Rudolf Nureyev and Margot Fonteyn became the greatest ballet duo of all time. For such delights, seats were top dollar—nearly £100—or just ¹⁄₂₀ of that lordly amount. London's premier opera venue was designed in 1858 by E. M. Barry, son of Sir Charles, the House of Commons architect. By now, the new ROH chief, New Yorker Michael Kaiser, should have set in motion his wish to cut ticket prices and bring opera to the masses. Kaiser's aim is that the new house should be more than just a concert hall and host a greater variety of performing troupes and events. If his efforts bear fruit, many critics hope Londoners pack the house and give the ROH administrators deserving applause—and not a repeat performance of 1763, 1792, and 1809, when riots broke out as the cost of rebuilding inflated the price of admission. But top prices are almost worth it if you can enjoy the house's Crush Bar, which adds opulence to the pastime of people-watching during an intermission. Call for current updates on the performing schedule of the troupes; for further information, *see* The Arts *in* Chapter 5. ⊠ *Bow St.,* ☎ *020/7240–1066 or 020/ 7240-1200. Tube: Covent Garden.*

🕐 ❻ The **Theatre Museum** aims to re-create the excitement of theater itself. There are usually programs in progress allowing children to get in a mess with makeup or have a giant dressing-up session. Permanent exhibits attempt a history of the English stage, with artifacts from the 16th century to Mick Jagger's jumpsuit, and tens of thousands of theater playbills and sections on such topics as Hamlet-through-the-ages and pantomime. ⊠ *7 Russell St.,* ☎ *020/ 7836–7891.* 🔄 *£3.50.* ⊙ *Tues.–Sun. 11–7. Tube: Covent Garden.*

Bloomsbury and Legal London

The character of an area of London can change visibly from one street to the next. Nowhere is this so clear as in the contrast between fun-loving Soho and intellectual Bloomsbury, a mere 100 yards to the northeast, or between arty, trendy Covent Garden and—on the other side of Kingsway— sober Holborn. Both Bloomsbury and Holborn are almost purely residential and should be seen by day. The first district is best known for its famous flowering of literary-arty bohemia, personified by the clique known as the Bloomsbury Group during this century's first three decades, and for the British Museum and the University of London, which dominate it now. The second sounds as exciting as, say, a center for accountants or dentists, but don't be put off—filled with magnificently ancient buildings, it's more interesting and beautiful than you might suppose.

Most travelers head here to find the ghosts of all those great Bloomsbury figures such as Virginia Woolf, E. M. Forster, Vanessa Bell, and Lytton Strachey. Ghosts of their literary salons soon lead into the time-warp territory of interlocking alleys, gardens and cobbled courts, town houses and halls where London's legal profession grew up. The Great Fire of 1666 razed most of the city but spared the buildings of legal London, and the whole neighborhood—known as Holborn—oozes history. Leading landmarks here are the Inns of Court, where the country's top solicitors and barristers have had their chambers for centuries.

Numbers in the text correspond to numbers in the margin and on the Bloomsbury and Legal London map.

Sights to See

① **British Library.** Since 1759, the British Library had always been housed in the British Museum on Gordon Square—but space ran out long ago, necessitating this grand new edifice, a few blocks north of the British Museum, between Euston and St. Pancras stations. The great exodus of 18 million volumes is almost complete, and by June 1999 the building will be fully operational. Happily, the library's treasures are already on view to the general public: the Magna Carta, a Gutenberg Bible, Jane Austen's writings, Shakespeare's First Folio, and musical manuscripts by Handel and Sir Paul McCartney are on show in the John Ritblat Gallery. ✉ *96 Euston Rd., ☎ 020/7412-7000. ⊡ Free. ☉ Mon.–Sat. 10–5, Sun. 2:30–6. Tube: Holborn or Tottenham Court Rd.*

★ ④ ℭ **British Museum.** With a facade like a great temple, this celebrated treasure house—filled with plunder of incalculable value and beauty from around the globe—is housed in a ponderously dignified Greco-Victorian building that makes a suitably grand impression. This is only appropriate, for inside you'll find some of the greatest relics of humankind: the Elgin Marbles, the Rosetta Stone, the Ur Treasure—everything, it seems, but the Ark of the Covenant. The museum is rapidly shaking off its ponderous dust as a rash of new galleries open and sections are updated, particularly with the addition of collections from the now-closed Museum of Mankind. The focal point is the Great Court, a brilliant techno-classical design with a vast glass roof, which

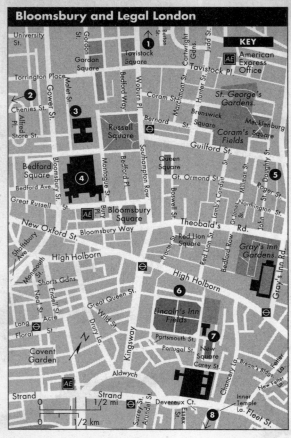

Bloomsbury and Legal London

British
Library, **1**

British
Museum, **4**

Dickens
House, **5**

Lincoln's
Inn, **7**

Pollock's Toy
Museum, **2**

Sir John
Soane's
Museum, **6**

Temple, **8**

University of
London, **3**

Finally, a travel companion that doesn't snore on the plane or eat all your peanuts.

When traveling, your MCI WorldCom Card is the best way to keep in touch. Our operators speak your language, so they'll be able to connect you back home—no matter where your travels take you. Plus, your MCI WorldCom Card is easy to use, and even earns you frequent flyer miles every time you use it. When you add in our great rates, you get something even more valuable: peace-of-mind. So go ahead. Travel the world. MCI WorldCom just brought it a whole lot closer.

You can even sign up today at www.mci.com/worldphone or ask your operator to make a collect call to 1-410-314-2938.

EASY TO CALL WORLDWIDE

1 **Just dial the WorldPhone access number of the country you're calling from.**
2 **Dial or give the operator your MCI WorldCom Card number.**
3 **Dial or give the number you're calling.**

Argentina	
To call using Telefonica	0-800-222-6249
To call using Telecom	0-800-555-1002
Brazil	**000-8012**
France ◆	**0-800-99-0019**
Ireland	**1-800-55-1001**
United Kingdom	
To call using BT	0800-89-0222
To call using CWC	0500-89-0222
United States	**1-800-888-8000**

For your complete WorldPhone calling guide, dial the WorldPhone access number for the country you're in and ask the operator for Customer Service. In the U.S. call 1-800-431-5402.

◆ Public phones may require deposit of coin or phone card for dial tone.

EARN FREQUENT FLYER MILES

American Airlines
AAdvantage

Continental Airlines
OnePass

Delta Air Lines
SkyMiles

MILEAGE PLUS
United Airlines

US AIRWAYS
DIVIDEND MILES

MCI WorldCom, its logo and the names of the products referred to herein are proprietary marks of MCI WorldCom, Inc. All airline names and logos are proprietary marks of the respective airlines. All airline program rules and conditions apply.

The first thing you need overseas is the one thing you forget to pack.

FOREIGN CURRENCY DELIVERED OVERNIGHT

Chase Currency To Go® delivers foreign currency to your home
by the next business day*

It's easy—before you travel, call
1-888-CHASE84 for delivery of any
of 75 currencies

Delivery is free with orders of
$500 or more

Competitive rates—
without exchange fees

You don't have to be a Chase
customer—you can pay by Visa®
or MasterCard®

 CHASE

THE RIGHT RELATIONSHIP IS EVERYTHING.®

1•888•CHASE84
www.chase.com

highlights and reveals the museum's best-kept secret—an inner courtyard—for the first time in 150 years. New galleries and exhibit space will celebrate the museum's 250th birthday in 2003 and bring it bang into the new century. Beyond the new frontage, there are 2½ mi of floor space inside, split into nearly 100 galleries—so arm yourself with a free floor plan directly as you go in, or they'll have to send out search parties to rescue you.

The collection began in 1753 and grew quickly, thanks to enthusiastic kleptomaniacs during the Napoleonic Wars—most notoriously the seventh Earl of Elgin, who lifted marbles from the Parthenon and Erechtheum while on a Greek vacation between 1801 and 1804. Here follows a highly edited résumé (in order of encounter) of the BM's greatest hits: close to the entrance hall, in the south end of Room 25, is the **Rosetta Stone,** found in 1799, and carved in 196 BC with a decree of Ptolemy V in Egyptian hieroglyphics, demotic, and Greek. It was this multilingual inscription that provided the French Egyptologist Jean-François Champollion with the key to deciphering hieroglyphics. Maybe the **Elgin Marbles** ought to be back in Greece, but since they are here—and they are, after all, among the most graceful and heartbreakingly beautiful sculptures on earth—make a beeline for them in Room 8, west of the entrance in the Parthenon Galleries, opened in June 1998. The best part is what remains of the Parthenon frieze that girdled the cella of Athena's temple on the Acropolis, carved around 440 BC. Also in the West Wing is one of the Seven Wonders of the Ancient World—in fragment form, unfortunately—in Room 12: the **Mausoleum of Halicarnassus.**

Upstairs are some of the most perennially popular galleries, especially beloved by children: Rooms 60 and 61, where the **Egyptian mummies** live. Nearby are the glittering 4th-century Mildenhall Treasure and the equally splendid Sutton Hoo Treasure. A more prosaic exhibit is that of Pete Marsh, sentimentally named by the archaeologists who unearthed the Lindow Man from a Cheshire peat marsh; poor Pete was ritually slain, probably as a human sacrifice. ⊠ *Great Russell St., WC1,* ☎ *020/7636–1555 or 020/7580–1788.* 🖾 *Free (suggested donation of £2. Guided tours: check at the information desk for details).* ☉ *Mon.–*

Sat. 10–5, Sun. noon–6. Tube: Tottenham Court Rd., Holborn, Russell Sq.

⑤ Dickens House. This is the only one of the many London houses Dickens inhabited that's still standing, and it would have had a real claim to his fame in any case, since he wrote *Oliver Twist* and *Nicholas Nickleby* and finished *Pickwick Papers* here between 1837 and 1839. The house looks exactly as it would have in Dickens's day, complete with first editions, letters, and tall clerk's desk, plus a treat for Lionel Bart fans—his score of *Oliver!* ⊠ *48 Doughty St.,* ☎ *020/7405–2127.* ⚏ *£3.50.* ☻ *Weekdays 9:45–5:30; Sat. 10–5. Closed Dec. 24–Jan. 1. Tube: Russell Sq.*

⑦ Lincoln's Inn. One of the oldest, best preserved, and most comely of the Inns of Court, Lincoln's Inn offers plenty to see—from the Chancery Lane Tudor brick gatehouse to the wide-open, tree-lined, atmospheric Lincoln's Inn Fields and the 15th-century Chapel remodeled by Inigo Jones in 1620. The wisteria-clad New Square is London's only complete 17th-century square. ⊠ *Chancery La.,,* ☎ *020/7405–1393.* ☻ *Gardens and chapel weekdays 12:30–2:30; guided tours available. Tube: Chancery Lane.*

☙ ② Pollock's Toy Museum. Historians tell us that the Victorians invented the concept of childhood, and no better proof can be offered than this magical place, a treasure trove of a small museum in a 19th-century town house. Most of the objects are dolls, dolls' houses, teddy bears, folk toys—and those bedazzling mementos of Victorian childhood, Pollock's famed cardboard cutout miniature theaters, all red velvet and gold trim, with movable scenery and figurines. Happily, Pollock's still sells these toy theaters—a souvenir that will drive both children and connoisseurs mad with joy. ⊠ *1 Scala St.,* ☎ *020/7636–3452.* ⚏ *£2.50.* ☻ *Mon.–Sat. 10–5. Tube: Goodge St.*

★ ⑥ Sir John Soane's Museum. Guaranteed to raise a smile from the most blasé and footsore tourist, this beloved collection hardly deserves the burden of its dry name. Sir John, architect of the Bank of England, who lived here from 1790 to 1831, created one of London's most idiosyncratic and fascinating houses. Everywhere mirrors and colors play tricks with light and space, and split-level floors worthy of a fairground fun house disorient you. In a basement chamber sits the vast 1300 BC sarcophagus of Seti I, lit by a domed skylight two stories above. ⊠ *13 Lincoln's Inn Fields,* ☎ *020/7405–2107.* ☜ *Free.* ☉ *Tues.–Sat. 10–5; until 9 on the first Tues. of every month. Tube: Holborn.*

❽ Temple. This is the collective name for **Inner Temple** and **Middle Temple,** and its entrance—the exact point of entry into the City—is marked by a young (1880) bronze griffin, the **Temple Bar Memorial.** In the buildings opposite is an elaborate stone arch through which you pass into Middle Temple Lane, past a row of 17th-century timber-frame houses, and on into Fountain Court. If the Elizabethan **Middle Temple Hall** is open, don't miss its hammer-beam roof—among the finest in the land. There is no admission charge, but a tip should be given to the porter. ⊠ *2 Plowden Buildings, Middle Temple,* ☎ *020/7427–4800.* ☉ *Weekdays 10–11:30 and (when not in use) 3–4. Tube: Temple.*

❸ University of London. A relatively youthful institution that grew out of the need for a nondenominational center for higher education, the University of London was founded by Dissenters in 1826, with its first examinations held 12 years later. Jews and Roman Catholics were not the only people admitted for the first time to an English university—women were, too, though they had to wait 50 years (until 1878) to sit for a degree.

The City

When an Englishman tells you that he works in the City, he isn't being vague. He means the British equivalent of Wall Street. The City extends eastward from Temple Bar to the Tower of London, and north from the Thames to Chiswell Street. Despite its small size (it's known as the Square Mile), this area is the financial engine of Britain and one of the world's leading centers of trade. The City, however, is more than just London's Wall Street: it is also home to two of the city's most notable sights, the Tower of London and St. Paul's, one of the world's greatest cathedrals—truly, a case of the money changers encompassing the temple!

Twice, the City has nearly been wiped off the face of the earth. The Great Fire of 1666 necessitated a total reconstruction, in which Sir Christopher Wren had a big hand, contributing not only his masterpiece, St. Paul's Cathedral, but 49 additional parish churches. The second wave of destruction was dealt by the German bombers of World War II. The ruins were rebuilt, but slowly, and with no overall plan, leaving the City a patchwork of the old and the new, the interesting and the flagrantly awful. Since a mere 8,000 or so people call it home, the financial center of Britain is deserted outside the working week, with restaurants shuttered and streets forlorn and windswept.

Numbers in the text correspond to numbers in the margin and on The City map.

Sights to See

⑩ Bank of England. Known familiarly for the past couple of centuries as "The Old Lady of Threadneedle Street," the bank has been central to the British economy since 1694. Sir John Soane designed the Neoclassic hulk in 1788, wrapping it in windowless walls (which are all that survive of his building) to suggest a stability that the ailing economy of the post-Thatcher years tends to belie. ⊠ *Bartholomew La.,* ☎ *020/7601–5545.* ▨ *Free.* ☉ *Weekdays 10–5, and Lord Mayor's Show day. Tube: Bank, Monument.*

⑥ Barbican Centre. An enormous concrete maze Londoners love to hate, the Barbican is home to the Royal Shakespeare Company and its two theaters, the London Symphony Orchestra and its auditorium, the Guildhall School of Music and Drama, a major gallery for touring exhibitions, two cinemas, and a convention center. Londoners have come to accept the place, if not exactly love it, because of its contents. ⊠ *Silk St., EC2,* ☎ *020/7638–8891; 020/7628–3351 RSC backstage tour.* ▨ *Barbican Centre free, gallery £5..* ☉ *Barbican Centre Mon.–Sat. 9 am–11 pm, Sun. noon–11 pm; gallery Mon.–Sat. 10–7:30, Sun. noon–7:30; conservatory weekends noon–5:30 when not in use for private function (call first). Tube: Moorgate, Barbican.*

① Dr. Johnson's House. Samuel Johnson lived here between 1746 and 1759, while in the worst of health, compiling his famous dictionary in the attic. Like Dickens, he lived all

over town, but, like Dickens's House, this is the only
of Johnson's abodes remaining today. It is an appropriat
17th-century house, exactly the kind of place you woul
expect the Great Bear, as Johnson was nicknamed, to live
in. It is a shrine to the man possibly more attached to London than anyone else, ever, and it includes a first edition
of his dictionary among the Johnson-and-Boswell mementos. After soaking up the atmosphere, repair around
the corner in Wine Office Court to the famed Ye Olde
Cheshire Cheese pub, once Johnson and Boswell's favorite
watering hole. ⊠ *17 Gough Sq.,* ☎ *020/7353–3745.* ⊠
£3. ☺ *May–Sept., Mon.–Sat. 11–5:30; Oct.–Apr., Mon.–
Sat. 11–5. Tube: Chancery Lane, Temple.*

❾ Guildhall. In the symbolic nerve center of the City, the Cor-
poration of London ceremonially elects and installs its
Lord Mayor as it has done for 800 years. The Guildhall
was built in 1411, and though it failed to escape either the
1666 or 1940 flames, its core survived. The fabulous hall
is a psychedelic patchwork of coats of arms and banners
of the City Livery Companies. ⊠ *Gresham St.,* ☎ *020/7606–
3030.* ⊠ *Free.* ☺ *Weekdays 10–5 (library closed weekends).
Tube: St. Paul's, Moorgate, Bank, Mansion House.*

⑪ Lloyd's of London. Architect Richard Rogers's (of Paris's
Pompidou Centre fame) fantastical steel-and-glass medium-
rise of six towers around a vast atrium, with his trademark
inside-out ventilation shafts, stairwells, and gantries, may
be the most exciting recent structure London can claim. The
building housing the famous insurance agency is best seen
at night, when cobalt and lime spotlights make it leap out
of the deeply boring gray skyline, like Carmen Miranda dancing at a funeral. Since the firm nearly went bankrupt several years ago, the atrium gallery, once open to public view,
has been closed. ⊠ *1 Lime St.,* ☎ *020/7623–7100. Tube:
Eastcheap.*

⑫ Monument. Built to commemorate the "dreadful visita-
tion" of the Great Fire of 1666, this is the world's tallest
isolated stone column—the work of Wren. There is a viewing gallery (311 steps up—better for you than any Stair-
Master). ⊠ *Monument St.,* ☎ *020/7626–2717.* ⊠ *£1.* ☺
*Daily 10–5:40 (new opening times on trial period, phone
before visiting). Tube: Monument.*

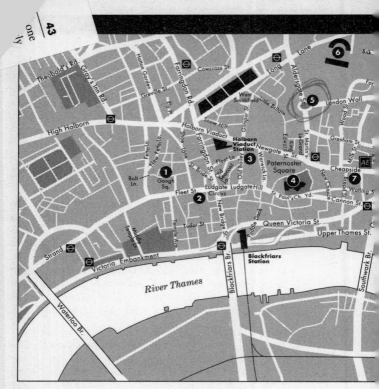

Bank of
England, **10**

Barbican
Centre, **6**

Dr. Johnson's
House, **1**

Guildhall, **9**

Lloyd's of
London, **11**

Monument, **12**

Museum of
London, **5**

Old Bailey, **3**

St. Bride's, **2**

St. Mary-le-
Bow, **7**

St. Paul's
Cathedral, **4**

Temple of
Mithras, **8**

Tower Bridge, **14**

Tower of
London, **13**

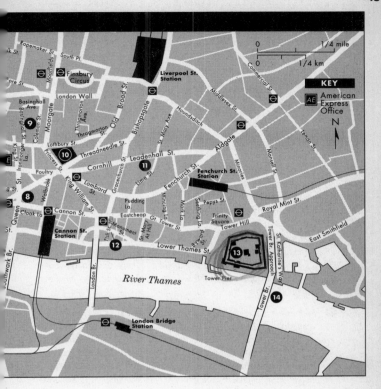

KEY

AE American
Express
Office

N

0   1/4 mile
0   1/4 km

Ropemaker St.   South Pl.

Finsbury
Circus

Liverpool St.
Station

London Wall

Basinghall
Ave.

Middlesex St.

Commercial St.

Moorgate

Houndsditch

Fore St.

Moorfields

London Wall

Throgmorton
St.

Throgmorton Ave.

Old Broad St.

Bishopsgate

St. Mary Axe

Aldgate

Leman St.

9

Coleman St.

Lothbury St.

10

Princes St.

Threadneedle St.

Cornhill

Leadenhall St.

11

Lime St.

Fenchurch St.
Station

Minories

Mansell St.

Poultry

Gracechurch St.

Fenchurch St.

Royal Mint St.

8

Lombard

King William St.

Mincing La.

Mark La.

Seething La.

Pepys St.

East Smithfield

Queen   Walbrook

Cloak La.

Cannon St.

Pudding
La.

Eastcheap

Gt. Tower St.

Trinity
Square

Tower Hill

St. Katharine's Way

Cannon St.
Station

Fish St. Hill

Monument
St.

St. Mary
At Hill

13

Tower Br. Approach

12

Lower Thames St.

Tower Pier

River Thames

London Br.

Southwark Br.

14

Tower Br.

London Bridge
Station

☞ ➎ **Museum of London.** Anyone with the least interest in how this city evolved will adore this museum, especially its reconstructions and dioramas—of the Great Fire (flickering flames! sound effects!), a 1940s air-raid shelter, a Georgian prison cell, and a Victorian street complete with fully stocked shops. Come right up to date in the new "London Now" gallery. ✉ *London Wall,,* ☎ *020/7600–0807.* ☞ *£5, free 4:30–5:50.* ☼ *Mon.–Sat. 10–5:50, Sun. noon–5:50. Tube: Barbican.*

➌ **Old Bailey.** The present-day Central Criminal Court is where legendary Newgate Prison stood from the 12th century right until the beginning of this one. Dickens visited Newgate several times (obviously in between pubs)—Fagin ended up in the Condemned Hold here in *Oliver Twist.* Ask the doorman which current trial is likely to prove juicy, if you're that kind of ghoul—you may catch the conviction of the next Crippen or Christie (England's most notorious wife murderers, both tried here). ✉ *Newgate St.,* ☎ *020/ 7248–3277.* ☞ *Free.* ☼ *Public Gallery weekdays 10–1 and 2–4; queue at the Newgate St. entrance. No cameras allowed. Tube: Blackfriars.*

➋ **St. Bride's.** One of the first of Wren's city churches, St. Bride's was also one of the bomb-damaged ones, reconsecrated only in 1960 after a 17-year-long restoration. From afar, study its extraordinary steeple—its uniquely tiered shape gave rise, legend has it, to the traditional wedding cake! ✉ *Fleet St.,* ☎ *020/7353–1301.* ☞ *Free.* ☼ *Mon.–Sat. 9–5, Sun. between services at 11 and 6:30. Tube: Chancery Lane.*

➐ **St. Mary-le-Bow.** This Wren church, dating from 1673, has one of the most famous sets of bells around—a Londoner must be born within the sound of Bow bells to claim to be a true cockney. The origin of that idea was probably the curfew rung on the bow Bells during the 14th century, even though "cockney" only came to mean Londoner three centuries later, and then it was an insult. In the crypt of the church you'll find The Place Below—a handy spot for great soups and quiches. Packed weekday lunchtimes, it's also open for breakfast, and Thursday and Friday evenings feature a posh vegetarian dinner. ✉ *Cheapside,* ☎ *020/7248–5139.* ☞ *Free.* ☼ *Mon.–Thurs. 6:30–6, Fri. 6:30–4. Tube: St. Paul's.*

★ ④ **St. Paul's Cathedral.** Often described as London's symbolic heart, St. Paul's is grand, stodgy, dirty, and enthralling.
The dome—the world's third largest—will already be familiar, since you see it peeping through on the skyline from
many an angle. The structure is, of course, Sir Christopher
Wren's masterpiece, completed in 1710 after 35 years of
building, then, much later, miraculously (mostly) spared by
World War II bombs. Wren's first plan, known as the New
Model, did not make it past the drawing board, while the
second, known as the Great Model, got as far as the 20-ft
oak rendering you can see here today before it also was re-
jected, whereupon Wren is said to have burst into tears. The
third, however, was accepted, with the fortunate coda that
the architect be allowed to make changes as he saw fit. Without that, there would be no dome, since the approved design had featured a steeple.

When you enter and see the dome from the inside, you may
find that it seems smaller than you expected. You aren't imag-
ining things; it *is* smaller, and 60 ft lower, than the lead-
covered outer dome. Beneath the lantern is Wren's famous
memorial, which his son composed and had set into the pave-
ment, and which reads succinctly: *Lector, si monumentum
requiris, circumspice*—"Reader, if you seek his monument,
look around you." Up 259 spiral steps is the **Whispering
Gallery,** an acoustic phenomenon; you whisper something
to the wall on one side, and a second later it transmits clearly
to the other side, 107 ft away. Ascend farther to the Stone
Gallery, which encircles the outside of the dome and affords
a spectacular panorama of London.

The poet John Donne, who had been dean of St. Paul's for
his final 10 years (he died in 1631), lies in the south choir
aisle. The vivacious choir-stall carvings nearby are the work
of Grinling Gibbons, as are the organ's, which Wren designed and Handel played. Behind the high altar, you'll find
the **American Memorial Chapel,** dedicated in 1958 to the
28,000 GIs stationed here who lost their lives in World War
II. ⊠ *St. Paul's Churchyard, EC4,* ☎ *020/7236–4128.* ▧
*Cathedral, ambulatory (American Chapel), crypt, and trea-
sury £4; galleries £3.50; combined ticket £7.50.* ⊘ *Cathedral Mon.–Sat. 8:30–4 (closed occasionally for special*

services); ambulatory, crypt, and galleries Mon.–Sat. 9:30–4:15. Tube: St. Paul's.

⑧ Temple of Mithras. Unearthed on a building site in 1954 and taken, at first, for an early Christian church, this was a minor place of pilgrimage in the Roman City. In fact, worshipers here favored Christ's chief rival, Mithras, the Persian god of light, during the 3rd and 4th centuries.

☝ ⑭ Tower Bridge. Despite its venerable, nay, medieval, appearance, this is a Victorian youngster that celebrated its centenary in June 1994. Constructed of steel, then clothed in Portland stone, it was deliberately styled in the Gothic persuasion to complement the Tower of London next door and is famous for its enormous bascules—the "arms," which open to allow large ships through, which is a rare occurrence these days. The bridge's 100th-birthday gift was a new exhibition, one of London's most imaginative and fun. You are conducted in the company of "Harry Stoner," an animatronic bridge construction worker worthy of Disneyland, back in time to witness the birth of the Thames's last downstream bridge. Be sure to hang on to your ticket and follow the signs to the Engine Rooms for part two, where the original steam-driven hydraulic engines gleam, and a cute rococo theater is the setting for an Edwardian music-hall production of the bridge's story. ☎ 020/7403–3761. 🎫 £6.15. ⊙ Apr.–Oct., daily 10–5:15; Nov.–Mar., daily 9:30–5:15 (last entry 1¼ hrs before closing). Tube: Tower Hill.

★ ⑬ Tower of London. Nowhere else does London's history come to life so vividly as in this minicity of melodramatic towers stuffed to bursting with heraldry and treasure, the intimate details of lords and dukes and princes and sovereigns etched in the walls (literally in some places, as you'll see), and quite a few pints of royal blood spilled on the stones. New systems ensure that lines are minimal, so you need no longer spend all day in line for the prize exhibit, the Crown Jewels, since they have been transplanted to a new home where moving walkways hasten progress at the busiest times.

The reason the Tower holds the royal gems is that it is still one of the royal palaces, although no monarch since Henry

VII has called it home. It has also housed the Royal Mint, the Public Records, the Royal Menagerie (which formed the basis of London Zoo), and the Royal Observatory, although its most renowned and titillating function has been, of course, as a jail and place of torture and execution.

A person was mighty privileged to be beheaded in the peace and seclusion of **Tower Green** instead of before the mob at Tower Hill. In fact, only seven people were ever important enough—among them Anne Boleyn and Catherine Howard, wives two and five of Henry VIII's six; Elizabeth I's friend Robert Devereux, Earl of Essex; and the nine-days' queen, Lady Jane Grey, age 17. In 1998, the executioner's block—with its bathetic forehead-size dent—and his axe, along with the equally famous rack and the more obscure "scavenger's daughter" (which pressed a body nearly to death), plus assorted thumbscrews, "iron maidens," and so forth, took up temporary residence in the newly opened collection of the Royal Armouries in Leeds, Yorkshire; after an undetermined time, they will return to the Royal Armouries collection of the Tower of London. Until then, fans of this horrifying niche of heavy metal might want to pay a call on the London Dungeon attraction, just across the Thames (☞ *below*).

Free tours depart every half hour or so from the Middle Tower. They are conducted by the 39 Yeoman Warders, better known as "Beefeaters"—ex-servicemen dressed in resplendent navy-and-red (scarlet-and-gold on special occasions) Tudor outfits. Beefeaters have been guarding the Tower since Henry VII appointed them in 1485. One of them, the Yeoman Ravenmaster, is responsible for making life comfortable for the Tower ravens—an important duty, since if Hardey, George, Hugine, Mumin, Cedric, Odin, Thor, and Gwylem (who talks) were to desert the Tower, goes the legend, the kingdom would fall. Today, the Tower takes no chances: the ravens' wings are cut.

In prime position stands the oldest part of the Tower and the most conspicuous of its buildings, the **White Tower.** Henry III (1207–1272) had it whitewashed, which is where the name comes from. The spiral staircase is the only way up, and here you'll find the **Royal Armouries,** Britain's national museum of arms and armor, with about 40,000 pieces on display. Most of the interior of the White Tower has been much altered over the centuries, but the **Chapel of St. John the Evangalist,** downstairs from the armouries, is a pure example of 11th-century Norman—very rare, very simple, and very beautiful. Across the moat, **Traitors' Gate** lies to the right. Immediately opposite Traitors' Gate is the former Garden Tower, better known since about 1570 as the **Bloody Tower.** Its name comes from one of the most famous unsolved murders in history, the saga of the "little princes in the Tower." In 1483 the uncrowned boy king, Edward V, and his brother Richard were left here by their uncle, Richard of Gloucester, after the death of their father, Edward I. They were never seen again, Gloucester was crowned Richard III, and in 1674 two little skeletons were found under the stairs to the White Tower. The obvious conclusions have always been drawn—and were, in fact, even before the skeletons were discovered.

The most dazzling, expensive, and absolutely the most famous exhibits here are, of course, the **Crown Jewels,** now housed in the new **Jewel House, Waterloo Block.** In their new settings you get so close to the fabled gems you feel you could polish them (if it weren't for the wafers of bulletproof glass), and they are enhanced by laser lighting, which nearly hurts the eyes with sparkle. Before you meet them in person, you are given a high-definition-film preview that features scenes from Elizabeth's 1953 coronation. Security is as fiendish as you'd expect, since the jewels—even though they would be literally impossible for thieves to sell—are *so* priceless that they're not insured. However, they are polished every January by the crown jewelers. A brief résumé of the top jewels: finest of all is the Royal Sceptre, containing the earth's largest cut diamond, the 530-carat Star of Africa. This is also known as Cullinan I, having been cut from the South African Cullinan, which weighed 20 ounces when dug up from a De Beers mine at the beginning of the century. Another chip off the block, Cullinan II, lives on the Imperial State Crown that Prince Charles is due to wear at his coronation—the same one that Elizabeth II wore in her coronation procession; it had been made for Victoria's in 1838. The other most famous gem is the Koh-i-noor, or

"Mountain of Light," which adorns the Queen Mother's crown. When Victoria was presented with this gift horse in 1850, she looked it in the mouth, found it lacking in glitter, and had it chopped down to almost half its weight.

The little chapel of **St. Peter ad Vincula** can be visited only as part of a Yeoman Warder tour. The second church on the site, it conceals the remains of some 2,000 people executed at the Tower, Anne Boleyn and Catherine Howard among them.

One of the more evocative towers is **Beauchamp Tower,** built west of Tower Green by Edward I (1272–1307). It was soon designated as a jail for the higher class of miscreant, including Lady Jane Grey, who is thought to have added her Latin graffiti to the many inscriptions carved by prisoners that you can see here. Don't forget to stroll along the battlements before you leave; from them, you get a wonderful overview of the whole Tower of London. ⊠ *H.M. Tower of London,* ☎ *020/7709–0765.* ▤ *£8.50, small additional charge for Fusiliers Museum.* ☉ *Mar.–Oct., Mon.–Sat. 9–5, Sun. 10–5; Nov.–Feb., Tues.–Sat. 9–4, Sun.–Mon. 10–4 (the Tower closes one hour after last admission time and all internal buildings close 30 minutes after last admission). Yeoman Warder guided tours leave daily (subject to weather and availability) from Middle Tower, at no charge (but a tip is always appreciated), about every 30 mins until 3:30 in summer, 2:30 in winter. For tickets to Ceremony of the Keys (the locking of the main gates, nightly at 10), write well in advance;* **The Resident Governor and Keeper of the Jewel House,** ⊠ *Queen's House, H.M. Tower of London, EC3. Give your name, the dates you wish to attend (including alternate dates), and number of people (up to 7), and enclose a SASE. Tube: Tower Hill.*

OFF THE
BEATEN
PATH

JACK THE RIPPER'S LONDON – *Cor Blimey Guv'nor, Jack the Ripper woz here!* Several organizations offer tours of "Jack's London"—the (still) mean streets of the East End, the working-class neighborhood directly to the east of the City. Here, in 1888, the Whitechapel murders traumatized Victorian London. At the haunting hour, tour groups head out to Bucks Row and other notorious scenes-of-the-crime. **Original London Walks** (020/7624–3978) offers frequent tours leaving at 7 PM from the Tower Hill tube stop, while the Jack the Ripper Mystery Walk (020/8558-9446) departs at 8 PM from the Aldgate tube stop Wednesday and Sunday. Even with a large tour group, this can be a spooky and unforgettable experience.

The South Bank

That old and snide North London dig about needing a passport to cross the Thames is no longer heard now. For decades, natives never ventured beyond the watery curtain that divides the city in half; tourists, too, rarely troubled the area unless they were departing from Waterloo Station. Starting with the 1976 creation of the South Bank Centre, however, the South Bank—the riverside stretch between Waterloo Bridge and Hungerford Bridge—has been taken over by Culture with a capital and emphatically illuminated C. Today, developers and local authorities have expanded the South Bank's potential farther east with an explosion of attractions that is turning this once-neglected district into London's most happening new neighborhood. The Eighties brought renovations and innovations such as Gabriel's Wharf, London Bridge City, Hay's Galleria, and Butler's Wharf; the Nineties arrived, and so did such headline-making sights as the spectacular reconstruction of Shakespeare's Globe—the most famous theater in the world—the OXO Tower, and the London Aquarium. A host of new attractions are drawing even the most ardent Northeners across the great divide. The new adjunct branch of the Tate Gallery is the star attraction. Perhaps in keeping with Britain's most renowned new artist, Damien Hirst (who often uses utensils and other found objects), this art center takes something functional—a 1930s power station—and makes it a place for inspiration and creativity. Over at the South Bank Centre, the world's largest Ferris wheel, officially called the British Airways London Eye, will give visitors a moment's flight over the city. Clearly, the South Bank has become a dazzling perch for culture vultures.

Actually, it is fitting that so much of London's artistic life should once again be centered here on the South Bank— back in the days of Ye Olde London Towne, Southwark was

the location for the theaters, taverns, and cock-⌐
arenas that served as after-hours entertainment. The ⌐
Theatre, in which Shakespeare acted and held shares, w
one of several established here; in truth, the Globe was as
likely to stage a few bouts of bearbaiting as the latest in-
terpretations of Shakespeare. Today, at the reconstructed
"wooden O," of course, you can just see the latter. Be sure
to take a walk along Bankside—the embankment along the
Thames from Southwark to Blackfriars Bridge—for fabulous vistas of London's skyline.

*Numbers in the text correspond to numbers in the margins
and on the South Bank map.*

Sights to See

⑤ British Airways London Eye. If you want a pigeon's-eye view
of London, this is the place to get it. The highest observa-
tion wheel in the world, this 500-ft Ferris wheel will tower
over the South Bank from the Jubliee Gardens next to
County Hall when it opens in January 2000. For 25 minutes, passengers hover over the city in a slow-motion flight,
so this won't be for the faint-hearted. ⊠ *Jubilee Gardens,
SE1.* ☜ *£6.95.* ☉ *Apr.–Oct. 9–sunset; Nov.–Mar. 10–6.*

㉑ Butler's Wharf. An '80s development that is maturing
gracefully, Butler's Wharf has many empty apartments in
its deluxe loft-style warehouse conversions and swanky
office blocks, but there *is* life here, thanks partly to London's saint of the stomach, Sir Terence Conran (also responsible for high-profile central London restaurants
Bibendum, Mezzo, and Quaglino's). He gave it his "Gas-
trodrome" of four restaurants, a vintner's, a deli, a bak-
ery, and who knows what else by now.

⑭ The Clink. The prison attached to Winchester House, palace
of the Bishops of Winchester until 1626, its name still
serves as a general term for jail. This was one of the first
prisons to detain women, most of whom were "Winchester Geese"—a euphemism meaning prostitutes. The oldest
profession was endemic in Southwark and now there is, of
all things, a museum tracing the history of prostitution here,
showing what the Clink was like during its 16th-century
scandalous heyday. ⊠ *1 Clink St.,* ☎ *020/7403–6515.* ☜
£4. ☉ *Daily 10–6. Tube: London Bridge.*

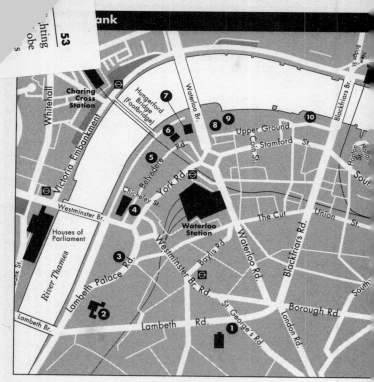

British Airways London Eye, **5**	*Golden Hinde*, **13**	London Dungeon, **18**	Royal Festival Hall, **6**
Butler's Wharf, **21**	Hays Galleria, **19**	Museum of the Moving Image (MOMI), **7**	Royal National Theatre, **9**
The Clink, **14**	HMS *Belfast*, **20**		Shakespeare's Globe
Design Museum, **22**	Imperial War Museum, **1**	Old St. Thomas's Operating Theatre, **17**	Theatre, **12**
Florence Nightingale Museum, **3**	Lambeth Palace, **2**	OXO Tower, **10**	South Bank Centre, **8**
	London Aquarium, **4**		

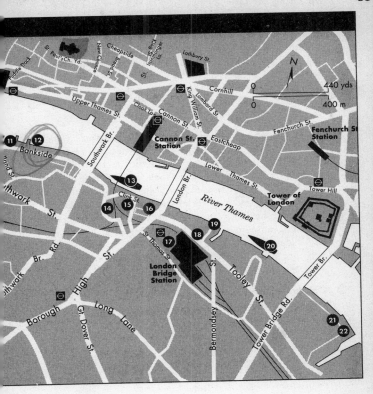

Southwark
Cathedral, **16**

Tate Gallery of
Modern Art,
Bankside, **11**

Vinopolis, **15**

㉒ Design Museum. Opened in 1989, this was the first museum in the world to elevate the everyday design we take for granted to the status of art exhibit, slotting it into its social and cultural context. The top floor traces the evolution of mass-produced goods. Check out the very good Blueprint Café, with its own river terrace. ⊠ *Butler's Wharf,* ☎ *020/7403–6933.* ▨ *£5.25.* ☉ *Daily 10:30–5:30. Tube: Tower Hill, then walk across river.*

❸ Florence Nightingale Museum. Here you can learn all about that most famous of health care reformers, "The Lady with the Lamp." On view are fascinating reconstructions of the barracks ward at Scutari (Turkey), where she tended soldiers during the Crimean War (1854–1856) and earned her nickname, and a Victorian East End slum cottage, to show what she did to improve living conditions among the poor. The museum is in St. Thomas's Hospital. ⊠ *2 Lambeth Palace Rd.,* ☎ *020/7620–0374.* ▨ *£3.50.* ☉ *Tues.–Sun. and public holidays 10–4. Tube: Waterloo, or Westminster and walk over the bridge.*

⓭ *Golden Hinde.* Sir Francis Drake circumnavigated the globe in this little galleon, or one just like it anyway. This exact replica has now finished *its* 23-year, round-the-world voyage—much of it spent along American coasts both Pacific and Atlantic—and has settled here to continue its educational function. ⊠ *St. Mary Overie Dock,* ☎ *020/7403–0123.* ▨ *£2.30.* ☉ *At press time, schedule being revised; telephone to check hrs. Tube: Blackfriars.*

⓳ Hay's Galleria. Once known as "London's larder" because of the edibles sold here, it was reborn in 1987 as a Covent Gardenesque parade of bars and restaurants, offices, and shops, all weatherproofed by an arched glass atrium roof supported by tall iron columns. Inevitably, jugglers, string quartets, and crafts stalls abound.

✇ ⓴ HMS *Belfast.* At 656 ft, this is one of the largest and most powerful cruisers the Royal Navy has ever had. It played a role in the D-Day landings off Normandy. There's an outpost of the Imperial War Museum on board. ⊠ *Morgan's La., Tooley St.,* ☎ *020/7940–6434.* ▨ *£4.70.* ☉ *Mid-Mar.–Oct., daily 10–6, Nov.–mid-Mar., daily 10–4:15.*

❶ Imperial War Museum. Housed in an elegantly colonnaded 19th-century building that was once the home of the infamous insane asylum called Bedlam, this museum of 20th-century warfare does not glorify bloodshed but attempts to evoke what it was like to live through the two world wars. Of course, there is hardware—a Battle of Britain Spitfire, a German V2 rocket—but there is an equal amount of war art (John Singer Sargent to Henry Moore). One very affecting exhibit is the *Blitz Experience*, which is what it sounds like—a 10-minute taste of an air raid in a street of acrid smoke with sirens blaring and searchlights glaring. A permanent new Holocaust exhibition, funded from a generous lottery grant, will open in 2000. ⊠ *Lambeth Rd.*, ☎ *020/7416-5000.* ▣ *£5.* ⊘ *Daily 10–6. Tube: Lambeth North.*

❷ Lambeth Palace. The London residence of the Archbishop of Canterbury—the senior archbishop of the Church of England—since the 13th century is rarely open to the public, but you can admire the fine Tudor gatehouse. *Tube: Waterloo, or Westminster and walk over the bridge.*

🖐 ❹ London Aquarium. Until recently, County Hall was the name of this curved, colonnaded neoclassic hulk, which took 46 years (1912–1958; two world wars interfered) to build, since it was home to London's local government, the Greater London Council, until it disbanded in 1986. Now, after a £25-million injection, a three-level aquarium has been installed, full of incongruous sharks and stingrays, educational exhibits, and piscine sights previously unseen on these shores. Between here and the South Bank Centre is the former **Jubilee Gardens**, which is the site of the millennium Ferris wheel, to be installed by 2000. Even without the 500-ft rotating elevation, views of the Houses of Parliament and Westminster Bridge are fine from here. ⊠ *County Hall, Westminster Bridge Rd.*, ☎ *020/7401-3433.* ▣ *£7.* ⊘ *Sept.–May, weekdays 10–6, weekends 9:30–6; June–Aug., daily 9:30–7:30. Tube: Waterloo, or Westminster and walk over the bridge.*

🖐 ⑱ London Dungeon. Did you ever wonder what a disembowelment actually looks like? See it here. Preteens seem to adore this place, which, although the city's most gory, grisly, gruesome museum, is among London's top tourist attractions and usually has long lines. Here realistic wax-work people are subjected in graphic detail to all the historical horrors the Tower of London merely suggests. Tableaus depict famous bloody moments—like Anne Boleyn's decapitation, or the martyrdom of St. George—alongside the torture, murder, and ritual slaughter of more anonymous victims, all to a soundtrack of screaming, wailing, and agonized moaning. London's times of deepest terror—the Great Fire and the Great Plague—are brought to life, too. Needless to say, a whole section is devoted to Jack the Ripper. Tots should stay away. ⊠ *28–34 Tooley St.,* ☎ *020/7403–0606.* ▦ *£8.95.* ⊘ *Apr.–Sept., daily 10–5:30; Oct.–Mar., daily 10–4:30. Tube: London Bridge.*

☞ ❼ **Museum of the Moving Image (MOMI).** Attached to the National Film Theatre (NFT) underneath Waterloo Bridge—whose two movie theaters offer easily the best repertory programming in London—MOMI may be the most fun of all London's museums. The main feature is a history of cinema from 4,000-year-old Javanese shadow puppets to Spielbergian special effects, but the supporting program is even better, and it stars *you.* Actors dressed as John Wayne or Mae West or usherettes or chorus girls pluck you out of obscurity to read the TV news or audition for the chorus line or fly like Superman over the Thames. Needless to say, this is always a big hit with kids. A popular spot for lunch or dinner is the NFT cafeteria—especially the big wooden tables outside. ⊠ *South Bank Centre,* ☎ *020/7401–2636.* ▦ *£6.25; White Card accepted.* ⊘ *Daily 10–6 (last admission at 5). Tube: Waterloo.*

❶❼ **Old St. Thomas's Operating Theatre.** One of England's oldest hospitals stood here from the 12th century until the railway forced it to move in 1862. Today, its operating theater has been restored into an exhibition of early 19th-century medical practices: the operating table onto which the gagged and blindfolded patients were roped; the box of sawdust underneath for catching their blood; the knives, pliers, and handsaws the surgeons wielded; and—this was a theater-in-the-round—the spectators' seats. ⊠ *9A St. Thomas St.,* ☎ *020/7955–4791.* ▦ *£2.50.* ⊘ *Tues.–Sun. 10–4. Closed Dec. 15–Jan. 5. Tube: London Bridge.*

10 **OXO Tower.** Long a London landmark to the cognoscenti, this wonderful Art Deco tower has graduated from its former incarnations as power-generating station and warehouse into a vibrant community of artists' and designers' workshops, a pair of restaurants, and cafés, as well as five floors of the best low-income housing in the city, via a £20 million scheme by Coin Street Community Builders. There's a rooftop viewing gallery for the latest river vista in town, and a performance area on the ground (first) floor, which comes alive all summer long—as does the entire surrounding neighborhood. ⊠ *Bargehouse St.,* ☎ *020/7401–3610.* 🖃 *Free.* ☉ *Studios and shops Tues.–Sun. 11–6. Tube: Blackfriars or Waterloo.*

6 **Royal Festival Hall.** The largest auditorium of the South Bank Centre, this hall features superb acoustics and a 3,000-plus capacity. It is the oldest of the riverside blocks, raised as the centerpiece of the 1951 Festival of Britain, a postwar morale-boosting exercise. The London Philharmonic resides here; symphony orchestras from the world over like to visit; and choral works, ballet, serious jazz and pop, and even film with live accompaniment are also staged. There is a good, independently run restaurant, the People's Palace, and a very good bookstore. The next building you come to also contains two concert halls, the **Queen Elizabeth Hall** and the **Purcell Room.** ⊠ *South Bank Centre at South Bank,* ☎ *020/7928–8800. Tube: Waterloo or Embankment.*

9 **Royal National Theatre.** Londoners generally felt the same way about Sir Denys Lasdun's Brutalist-style function-dictates-form building when it opened in 1976 as they would a decade later about the far nastier Barbican. But whatever its merits or demerits as a landscape feature, the Royal National Theatre—still abbreviated colloquially to the preroyal warrant "NT"—has wonderful insides. Three auditoriums—the Olivier, named after Sir Laurence, first artistic director of the National Theatre Company; the Lyttleton; and the Cottesloe—host an ever-changing array of presentations. The NT does not rest on its laurels. It attracts many of the nation's top actors (Anthony Hopkins, for one, does time here) in addition to launching future stars. ⊠ *South Bank,*

☎ 020/7452–3000 box office. ⊙ Foyers Mon.–Sat. 10 am–11 pm; hr-long backstage tours (£4.25) Mon.–Sat. at 10:15, 12:30, and 5:30. Tube: Waterloo.

★ ⑫ **Shakespeare's Globe Theatre.** Three decades ago, American Sam Wanamaker—then an aspiring actor—pulled up in Southwark in a cab and was amazed to find that the fabled Shakespeare's Globe Theatre didn't actually exist. Worse: a tiny plaque was the only sign on the former site of the world's most legendary theater. So appalled had he been that London lacked a center for the study and worship of the Bard of Bards, Wanamaker worked ceaselessly until his death in 1993 to raise funds for his dream—a full-scale reconstruction of the theater. The dream was realized in 1996 when an exact replica of Shakespeare's open-roof Globe Playhouse (built in 1599; incinerated in 1613) was created, using authentic Elizabethan materials and craft techniques and the first thatched roof in London since the Great Fire. Scheduled to open by summer 2000 will be a second, indoor theater, built to a design of the 17th-century architect Inigo Jones. The whole theater complex stands 200 yards from the original Globe, the famous "Wooden O." Today, a repertory season of four Shakespeare plays is presented during the summer—usually mid-May to late September—in natural light (and sometimes rain), to 1,000 people on wooden benches in the "bays," plus 500 "groundlings," standing on a carpet of filbert shells and clinker, just as they did nearly four centuries ago. For any theater buff, this stunning project is a must. Although the main theater is open only for performances during the summer season, it can be viewed year-round if you take the helpful tour provided by the **New Shakespeare's Globe Exhibition,** touted as the largest ever to focus on Shakespeare, his work, and his contemporaries; this all-singing, all-dancing exhibition is housed in the Undercroft, beneath the Globe site. ⊠ New Globe Walk, Bankside, ☎ 020/7902–1500. 🎟 Exhibition £5. ⊙ Daily 10–5; call for performance schedule. Tube: Mansion House, then walk across Southwark Bridge.

⑧ **South Bank Centre.** On either side of Waterloo Bridge is London's chief arts center. Along Upper Ground, you'll first reach the **Royal National Theatre** (☞ above)—three auditoriums that are home to some of the finest theater in Britain. Underneath Waterloo Bridge is the **National Film Theatre**—the best repertory cinema house in London—and its most intriguing attraction, the **Museum of the Moving Image** (**MOMI**) (☞ *above*). Also here are the **Royal Festival Hall** (☞ *above*), the **Queen Elizabeth Hall** and the **Purcell Room**—three of London's finest venues for classical music. Finally, tucked away behind the concert halls is the **Hayward Gallery**, a venue for impressive, ever-changing art exhibitions. Along the wide paths of the complex you'll find distractions of every sort—secondhand bookstalls, entertainers, and arrogant pigeons. ⊠ *South Bank Centre,* ☎ *020/7401–2636. Tube: Waterloo.*

16 **Southwark Cathedral.** This cathedral (pronounced *suth*-uck) is the second-oldest Gothic church in London, next to Westminster Abbey. Look for the gaudily renovated 1408 tomb of the poet John Gower, friend of Chaucer, and for the Harvard Chapel, named after John Harvard, founder of the American college, who was baptized here in 1608. Another notable buried here is Edmund Shakespeare, brother of William.

11 **Tate Gallery of Modern Art, Bankside.** This much anticipated new adjunct branch of the Tate Gallery is due to open in May 2000 in the Bankside Power Station. Shuttered for decades, the station has glowered magnificently on its Thamesside site ever since it was built in the 1930s. Now it has been renovated by Swiss architects Herzog & de Meuron to make a dazzling venue for some of the Tate's overflowing treasures. For decades, the old Millbank Gallery of the Tate (☞ *above*) had been so overstuffed the curators had to resort to a revolving menu of paintings and sculpture. The Power Station (designed by the same man who created the famous red telephone box) and its 8.5 acre site will now house the overflow, running from classic works by Matisse, Picasso, Dali, Moore, Bacon, and Warhol to the most-talked-about British artists of today. It promises to be one of the world's finest modern art museums and the most spectacular Millennium-year addition to London's art scene. ⊠ *25 Summer St., SE1 9JT,* ☎ *020/7887–8000.* ▨ *Free.* ☉ *Hours not determined at press time.*

⑮ Vinopolis. The Brits are perhaps not the first nation you would expect to erect a monument to wine, but here it is—Vinopolis, City of Wine. Spread over two acres between the Globe Theatre and London Bridge, its arched vaults promise multimedia tours of the world's wine cultures, tastings, retail shops, an art gallery, restaurants, and a wine school. ⊠ *Axe and Bottle Court, 70 Newcomen St.,* ☎ *020/7645–3700.* ▣ *£10.* ☉ *Mon.–Sat. 10–5:30.*

Kensington, Knightsbridge, Mayfair, Belgravia, and Hyde Park

Even in these supposedly democratic days, you still sometimes hear people say that the *only* place to live in London is in the grand residential area of the Royal Borough of Kensington. True, the district is an endless cavalcade of streets lined with splendid houses redolent of stuccoed wealth and pillared porches, but there are other fetching attractions here—some of the most fascinating museums in London, stylish squares, elegant antiques shops, and Kensington Palace, the former home of both Diana, Princess of Wales, and Queen Victoria, which put the district literally on the map back in the 17th century. To Kensington's east is one of the highest concentrations of important artifacts anywhere, the "museum mile" of South Kensington, with the rest of Kensington offering peaceful strolls, a noisy main street, and another palace. Kensington first became the *Royal* Borough of Kensington (and Chelsea) when William III, who suffered terribly from the Thames mists over Whitehall, decided in 1689 to buy Nottingham House in the rural village of Kensington so that he could breathe more easily. Courtiers and functionaries and society folk soon followed where the crowns led, and by the time Queen Anne was on the throne (1702–1714), Kensington was overflowing. In a way, it still is, since most of its grand houses have been divided into apartments, or else are serving as foreign embassies.

Now visitors enter Kensington Gardens to see Kensington Palace and to explore the parks themselves. Hyde Park and Kensington Gardens together form by far the biggest of central London's royal parks. It's probably been centuries since any major royal had a casual stroll here, but the parks remain the property of the Crown, and it was the Crown that saved them from being devoured by the city's late-18th-century growth spurt.

Around the western borders of Hyde Park are several of London's poshest and most beautiful neighborhoods. To the south of the park and just a short carriage ride from Buckingham Palace is the most splendidly aristocratic enclave to be found in London: Belgravia—this is *Upstairs, Downstairs* Eaton Square territory. Its stucco-white buildings and grand squares—particularly Belgrave Square—are preserved Regency-era jewels. On the western border of Hyde Park is Mayfair, which gives Belgravia a definite run for its money as London's wealthiest district. Here are three mansions that will allow you to get a peek into the lifestyles of London's rich and famous—19th- and 20th-century versions: Apsley House, the home of the Duke of Wellington; Spencer House, home of Princess Diana's ancestors; and the Wallace Collection, a grand mansion on Manchester Square stuffed with great art treasures.

Numbers in the text correspond to numbers in the margin and on the Kensington, Knightsbridge, Mayfair, Belgravia, and Hyde Park map and the Regent's Park Area map.

Sights to See

❼   **Albert Memorial.** Finished a year ahead of schedule, the sombre black statue of Prince Albert, Queen Victoria's consort, has been lavishly regilded to see in the new century. In fact, the entire George Gilbert Scott edifice had been painted black to deter its detection by Zeppelins during World War I. Albert's grieving widow, Queen Victoria, had this elaborate confection erected on the spot where his Great Exhibition had stood a mere decade before his early death, from typhoid, in 1861. ✉ *Reservations for tours* ☎ *020/7495–0916.* ▣ *£3. Tube: Knightsbridge.*

★ **❸** **Apsley House (Wellington Museum).** Once known, quite simply, as Number 1, London, this was celebrated as the best address in town. Built by Robert Adam in the 1770s and reopened in 1996 after a superlative renovation, this mansion was home to the celebrated conqueror of Napoléon, the Duke of Wellington, who lived here from the 1820s until

64

Kensington, Knightsbridge, Mayfair, Belgravia and

KEY

AE American Express Office

i Tourist Information

Hornton St.
Campden Hill
Phillimore Gdns.
Kensington Church St.
Holland St.
Stafford Ter.
Kensington High St.
Kensington Sq.
Abingdon Rd.
Allen St.
Earl's Court Rd.
Maloes Rd.
Pembroke Rd.
Cromwell Rd.
The Broad Walk
Kensington Rd.
The Flow
Palace Gate
Victoria Rd.
Gloucester Rd.
Cornwall Gdns.
Queen
Cromw
K

N

Albert Memorial, **7**

Apsley House (Wellington Museum), **13**

Belgrave Place, **3**

Harrods, **12**

Kensington Palace, **5**

Kensington Palace Gardens, **4**

Leighton House, **1**

Linley Sambourne House, **2**

Natural History Museum, **9**

Royal Albert Hall, **8**

Science Museum, **10**

Serpentine Gallery, **6**

Spencer House, **14**

Victoria and Albert Museum, **11**

Wallace Collection, **15**

The Serpentine

Hyde Park

Rotten Row

South Carriage Dr.

Knightsbridge

Kensington Gore

Prince Consort Rd.

Queensgate

Exhibition Rd.

Imperial College Rd.

Cromwell Gdns.

Thurloe Pl.

Thurloe St.

Harrington Rd.

Pelham St.

Kensington Gardens

Walk

gate

Rd.

The Ring

Ennismore Gdns.

Brompton Sq.

Brompton

Brompton Rd.

Brompton Rd.

Beauchamp Pl.

Hans Rd.

Walton St.

Lennox Gdns.

Cottage Pl.

0   440 yds

0   400 m

his death in 1852. The great Waterloo Gallery—scene of legendary dinners—is one of the most spectacular rooms in England. Not to be missed, in every sense, is the gigantic Canova statue of a nude (but fig-leafed) Bonaparte in the entry stairwell. The current Duke of Wellington still lives here. ⊠ *149 Piccadilly,* ☎ *020/7499–5676.* ⊡ *£4.50.* ☉ *Tues.–Sun. 11–5. Tube: Hyde Park Corner.*

☙ ⑱ **BBC Experience.** For those who have been weaned on a steady diet of Masterpiece Theatre presentations, the BBC is the greatest television producer in the world. These fans, and those of the BBC's countless other programs, will be happy to know that the BBC has just opened the doors of its own in-house museum, to celebrate the BBC's 75th anniversary. There's an audiovisual show that traces the BBC's history, an interactive section—want to try your hand at commentating on a sports game, presenting a weather forecast, or making your own director's cut of a segment of *East-Enders?*—and, of course, a massive gift shop. This museum will probably be deluged by crowds for the first few years—conveniently, admission is on a pre-booked and timed system. ⊠ *Broadcasting House, Portland Place, W1,* ☎ *0870/603–0304, 01222/55771 outside U.K.* ⊡ *Free.* ☉ *Daily 9:30–5:30. Tube: Oxford Circus.*

❸ **Belgrave Place.** One of the main arteries of Belgravia—London's swankiest neighborhood—Belgrave Place is lined with grand, imposing Regency-era mansions (now mostly embassies). Walk down this street from sylvan Belgrave Square toward Eaton Place to pass two of Belgravia's most beautiful mews—Eaton Mews North and Eccleston Mews, both fronted by grand Westminster-white rusticated entrances right out of a 19th-century engraving. There are few other places where London is both so picturesque and elegant.

☙ ⑫ **Harrods.** Just in case you hadn't noticed it, Harrods has its domed terra-cotta Edwardian bulk outlined in thousands of white lights at night. The 15-acre Egyptian-owned store's sales weeks are world-class, and the environment is as frenetic as a stock-market floor. Don't miss the extravagant **Food Hall,** with its stunning art nouveau tiling in the neigh-

---

BBC
Experience,
18
London
Zoo, **16**
Madame
Tussaud's,
17

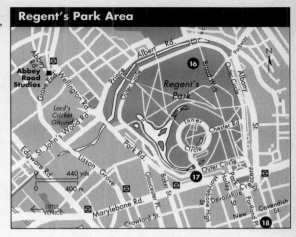

Regent's Park Area

borhood of meat and poultry. This is the department in which to acquire your green-and-gold-logo souvenir Harrods bag, since food prices are surprisingly competitive. ⊠ *87 Brompton Rd.,* ☎ *020/7730–1234. Tube: Knightsbridge.*

Hyde Park. Along with the smaller St. James's and Green parks to the east, Hyde Park started as Henry VIII's hunting grounds. Along its south side runs **Rotten Row,** still used by the Household Cavalry, who live at the **Knightsbridge Barracks**—a high-rise and a long, low, ugly red block to the left. This is the brigade that mounts the guard at the palace, and you can see them leave to perform this duty, in full regalia, at about 10:30, or see the exhausted cavalry return about noon.

Kensington Gardens. More formal than neighboring Hyde Park, Kensington Gardens was first laid out as palace grounds. The paved Italian garden at the top of the Long Water, **The Fountains** is a reminder of this, though, of course **Kensington Palace** itself is the main clue to its royal status, with its early 19th-century Sunken Garden north of it. Nearby is George Frampton's beloved 1912 *Peter Pan,* a bronze of the boy who lived on an island in the

Serpentine and never grew up, and whose creator, J. M. Barrie, lived at 100 Bayswater Road, not 500 yards from here. The **Round Pond** is a magnet for model-boat enthusiasts and duck feeders.

❺ Kensington Palace. Kensington was put, socially speaking, on the map when King William III, "much incommoded by the Smoak of the Coal Fires of London" decided in the 17th century to vacate Whitehall and relocate to a new palace outside the center city in the "village" of Kensington. The new palace did not enjoy a smooth passage as royal residence. Twelve years of renovation were needed before William and Mary could move in. Of course, royals have lived here since William and Mary—and some have died here, too. In 1760, poor George II burst a blood vessel while on the toilet (the official line was, presumably, that he was on the throne). The State Rooms where Victoria had her ultrastrict upbringing have recently been completely renovated, and they depict the life of the royal family through the past century. This palace is an essential stop for royalty vultures, because it's the only one where you may actually catch a glimpse of the real thing. Princess Margaret, the Duke and Duchess of Gloucester, and Prince and Princess Michael of Kent all have apartments here, as did, Diana, Princess of Wales, until her tragic death. Now, one hundred years after Queen Victoria and just a couple post-Diana, the palace has found new life in the shape of the **Royal Ceremonial Dress Collection,** which has recently reopened. Extending back centuries, the collection shows an array of state and occasional dresses, hats, and shoes worn by Britain's Royal Family. Diana-watchers will note the difference between the regal if dowdy garments of Her Majesty the Queen compared to the glittering, cutting-edge fashions of her daughter-in-law (although hasn't anybody noticed that Elizabeth is sporting more and more fashionable outfits these days?). Repair to the palace's nearby Orangery for an elegant pot of Earl Grey. ⊠ *The Broad Walk, Kensington Gardens, W8,* ☎ *020/7937–9561.* ▭ *£7.50, including admission to dress collection.* ⊘ *May–Oct., daily 10–5; Oct.–Mar., daily 10–3. Tube: High Street Kensington.*

❹ Kensington Palace Gardens. Immediately behind Kensington Palace is Kensington Palace Gardens (called Palace

Green at the south end), a wide, leafy avenue of mid-19th-century mansions that used to be one of London's most elegant addresses. Today, it's largely Embassy Row, including those of Russia and Israel. *Tube: High Street Kensington.*

❶ Leighton House. The exotic richness of late 19th-century aesthetic tastes is captured in this fascinating home, once the abode of Lord Leighton, the Victorian painter par excellence. The Arab Hall is lavishly lined with Persian tiles and pieced woodwork. Thanks to the generosity of John Paul Getty II, the somewhat neglected property has undergone a full renovation. Its neighborhood was one of the principal artists' colonies of Victorian London. If you are interested in domestic architecture of the 19th century, wander through the surrounding streets. ✉ *14 Holland Park Rd.,* ☎ *020/7602–3316.* 🎟 *Free.* ⊙ *Mon.–Sat. 11–5:30. Tube: Holland Park.*

★ ❷ Linley Sambourne House. On the eastern side of the Commonwealth Institute, discover this delightful Victorian residence, built and furnished in the 1870s by Mr. Sambourne, for more than 30 years the political cartoonist for the satirical magazine *Punch.* Stuffed with delightful Victorian and Edwardian antiques, fabrics, and paintings, this is one of the most charming 19th-century London houses extant—little wonder it was filmed for Merchant/Ivory's *A Room with a View.* ✉ *18 Stafford Terr.,* ☎ *020/8944–1019.* 🎟 *£3.* ⊙ *Mar.–Oct., Wed. 10–4, Sun. 2–5. Tube: High Street Kensington.*

🐾 ⓰ London Zoo. The zoo has been open for more than 150 years and peaked in popularity during the 1950s, but it recently faced the prospect of closing its gates forever. The animal-crazy Brits, apparently anxious about the morality of caging wild beasts, simply stopped visiting. In the '90s, the zoo fought back and now has corporate sponsorship and a great big modernization program. So successful has the zoo's revival been that it has now glitteringly expanded to include The Web of Life—a conservation and education center set in a spanking new glass pavilion. ✉ *Regent's Park, NW1,* ☎ *020/7722–3333.* 🎟 *£9.* ⊙ *Mar.–Oct. daily 10–5:30; Oct.–Feb. daily 10–4; pelican feed daily 1; aquarium feed daily 2:30; reptile feed Fri. 2:30; elephant bath daily 3:45. Tube: Camden Town, and Bus 74.*

⑰ Madame Tussaud's. This is nothing more, nothing less, than the world's premier exhibition of lifelike waxwork models of celebrities. Madame T. learned her craft while making death masks of French Revolution victims and in 1835 set up her first show of the famous ones near this spot. You can see everyone from Shakespeare to Benny Hill here, but top billing still goes to the murderers in the Chamber of Horrors, who stare glassy-eyed at you—this one from the electric chair, that one next to the tin bath where he dissolved several wives in quicklime. Just next door is the London Planetarium, which offers a special combo ticket with Tussaud's. Warning: the lines here can be ridiculous. ⊠ *Marylebone Rd., NW1,* ☎ *020/7935–6861.* 🎟 *£9.75, joint ticket with planetarium £12.* ⊘ *Sept.–June, weekdays 10–5:30, weekends 9:30–5:30; July–Aug., daily 9:30–5:30. Tube: Baker St.*

⑨ Natural History Museum. When you want to heed the call of the wild, discover this fun place—enter to find Dinosaurs on the left and the Ecology Gallery on the right. Both these exhibits (the former with life-size moving dinosaurs, the latter complete with moonlit "rain forest") make essential viewing in a museum that realized it was getting crusty and has consequently invested millions overhauling itself in recent years. Don't miss the Creepy Crawlies Gallery, which features a nightmarish super-enlarged scorpion, yet ends up making tarantulas seem cute. ⊠ *Cromwell Rd.,* ☎ *020/7938–9123.* 🎟 *£6; free weekdays 4:30–5:50, weekends 5–5:50; White Card accepted.* ⊘ *Mon.–Sat. 10–5:50, Sun. 11–5:50. Tube: South Kensington.*

⑧ Royal Albert Hall. This famous theater was made possible by the Victorian public, who donated funds for the domed, circular 8,000-seat auditorium. More money was raised, however, by selling 1,300 future seats at £100 apiece—not for the first night alone, but for every night for 999 years. (Some descendants of those purchasers still use the seats.) The Albert Hall is best known and best loved for its annual July–September Henry Wood Promenade Concerts (the "Proms"), with bargain-price standing (or promenading, or sitting-on-the-floor) tickets sold on the night of the world-class classical concerts. ⊠ *Kensington Gore,* ☎ *020/7589–3203.* 🎟 *Admission varies according to event. Tube: South Kensington.*

In case you want to see the world.

At American Express, we're here to make your journey a smooth one. So we have over 1,700 travel service locations in over 130 countries ready to help. What else would you expect from the world's largest travel agency?

do more **Travel**

In case you want to be welcomed there.

We're here to see that you're always welcomed at establishments everywhere. That's why millions of people carry the American Express® Card – for peace of mind, confidence, and security, around the world or just around the corner.

do more

Cards

In case you're running low.

**We're here to help with more than 190,000 Express Cash
locations around the world. In order to enroll, just call
American Express at 1 800 CASH-NOW before you start
your vacation.**

do more

**Express
Cash**

And in case you'd rather be safe than sorry.

We're here with American Express® Travelers Cheques. They're the safe way to carry money on your vacation, because if they're ever lost or stolen you can get a refund, practically anywhere or anytime. To find the nearest place to buy Travelers Cheques, call 1 800 495-1153. Another way we help you do more.

do more AMERICAN EXPRESS

Travelers
Cheques

☺ ⑩ **Science Museum.** Standing behind the Natural History Museum, this features loads of hands-on exhibits. Highlights include the Launch Pad gallery; the Computing Then and Now show; *Puffing Billy,* the oldest train in the world; and the actual *Apollo 10* capsule. The newest attraction is the Wellcome Wing, a new £45-million addition devoted to contemporary science, medicine, and technology, which also includes a 450-seat IMAX cinema. ⊠ *Exhibition Rd., SW7,* ☎ *020/7938–8000.* 🎫 *£6.50.* ☉ *Mon.–Sat. 10–6, Sun. 11–6. Tube: South Kensington.*

⑥ **Serpentine Gallery.** A gallery influential on the trendy art circuit, this place hosts temporary shows of modern work, often very avant-garde indeed. It overlooks the west bank of the **Serpentine,** a beloved lake, much frequented in summer, when the south shore Lido resembles a beach and the water is dotted with rented rowboats. ⊠ *Kensington Gardens,* ☎ *020/7402–6075.* 🎫 *Free.* ☉ *Daily 10–6; closed Christmas wk. Tube: Lancaster Gate.*

★ ⑭ **Spencer House.** Ancestral abode of the Spencers—the family who gave us Princess Diana—this great mansion is perhaps the finest example of 18th-century elegance, on a domestic scale, extant in London. Superlatively restored by Lord Rothschild, the house was built in 1766 for the first Earl Spencer, heir to the first Duchess of Marlborough. James "Athenian" Stuart decorated the gilded State Rooms, including the Painted Room, the first completely Neoclassic room in Europe. The most ostentatious part of the house (and the Spencers—as witness the £40,000 diamond shoe buckles the first countess proudly wore—could be given to ostentation) is the florid bow-window of the Palm Room: covered with stucco palm trees, it conjures up both ancient Palmyra and modern Miami Beach. ⊠ *27 St. James's Place,* ☎ *020/7499–8620.* 🎫 *£6; children under 10 not admitted.* ☉ *Sun. 10:45–4:45 (guided tours only; tickets go on sale each Sunday at 10:30). Closed Aug., Jan. Tube: Green Park.*

★ ⑪ **Victoria & Albert Museum.** Recognizable by the copy of Victoria's Imperial Crown it wears on the lantern above the central cupola, this museum is always referred to as the V&A. It is a huge museum, showcasing the applied arts of all disciplines, all periods, all nationalities, and all tastes, and it is a wonderful, generous place in which to get lost. The collections are *so* all-encompassing that confusion is a hazard—one minute you're gazing on the Jacobean oak 12-ft-square four-poster Great Bed of Ware (one of the V&A's most prized possessions, given that Shakespeare immortalized it in *Twelfth Night*); the next, you're in the 20th-century end of the equally celebrated Dress Collection, coveting a Jean Muir frock you can actually buy at nearby Harrods. Prince Albert, Victoria's adored consort, was responsible for the genesis of this permanent version of the 1851 Great Exhibition, and his queen laid its foundation stone in her final public London appearance in 1899. The latest renovations include the Raphael Galleries, where seven massive cartoons the painter completed in 1516 for his Sistine Chapel tapestries are housed. Be sure to check out young designer Danny Lane's breathtaking glass balustrade in the Glass Gallery. The special-events program here is one of the most exciting in the world—unique lectures, dinners, and the Late View salons lure the young and trendy. If you want to rest your overstimulated eyes, head for the brick-walled V&A café; its Sunday Jazz Brunch is fast becoming a London institution. ⊠ *Cromwell Rd.,* ☎ *020/7938–8500.* ☞ *Suggested contribution £5; free after 4:30, except Wed.; White Card accepted.* ⊙ *Mon. noon–5:45, Tues.–Sun. 10–5:45; Wed. Late View 4:30–9:30. Tube: South Kensington.*

★ ⑮ **Wallace Collection.** Assembled by four generations of marquesses of Hertford, the Wallace Collection is important, exciting, undervisited—and free. As at the Frick Collection in New York, the setting here, Hertford House, is part of the show—a fine late-18th-century mansion. It was the eccentric fourth marquess who really built the collection, snapping up Bouchers, Fragonards, Watteaus, and Lancrets for a song (the French Revolution having rendered them dangerously unfashionable). The highlight is Fragonard's *The Swing,* which conjures up the 18th-century's let-them-eat-cake frivolity better than any other painting around. Don't forget to smile back at Frans Hals's *Laughing Cavalier* in the Big Gallery. ⊠ *Hertford House, Manchester Sq.,* ☎ *020/7935–0687.* ☞ *Free.* ⊙ *Mon.–Sat. 10–5, Sun. 2–5. Tube: Bond, Baker St.*

OFF THE
BEATEN
PATH

ABBEY ROAD STUDIOS – Strawberry Beatles Forever! Here, outside the legendary Abbey Road Studios, is the most famous zebra crossing in the world. Immortalized on the Beatles's *Abbey Road* album of 1969, this footpath is a spot beloved to countless Beatlemaniacs and baby boomers. Adjacent to the traffic crossing, at No. 3 Abbey Road, are the studios where the Beatles recorded their entire output, from "Love Me Do" on, including, most momentously, *Sgt. Pepper's Lonely Hearts Club Band* (early 1967). To see this and other Fab Four sites, **Original London Walks** offers two Beatles tours: "The Beatles In-My-Life Walk" and "The Beatles Magical Mystery Tour" (☎ 020/7624–3978). Abbey Road is in the elegant neighborhood of St. John's Wood, a 10-minute ride on the tube from central London. Take the Jubilee subway line to the St. John's Wood tube stop, head southwest three blocks down Grove End Road—and be prepared for a heart-stopping vista right out of Memory Lane.

Up and Down the Thames

Home to the Millennium Dome and a number of historical and maritime attractions, Greenwich—set on the Thames some 8 km (5 mi) east of central London—is an ideal destination for a day out. Sir Christopher Wren's Royal Naval College and Inigo Jones's Queen's House reach architectural heights; the Old Royal Observatory measures time for our entire planet; and the Greenwich Meridian divides the world in two—you can stand astride it with one foot in either hemisphere. The National Maritime Museum and the proud clipper ship *Cutty Sark* thrill seafaring types, and landlubbers can stroll the green acres of parkland that surround the buildings, the quaint 19th-century houses, and the weekend crafts and antiques markets. Meanwhile, upstream, the royal palaces and grand houses that dot the area were built not as town houses but as country residences with easy access to London by river, and Hampton Court Palace is the best and biggest of all.

New transport links to the Millennium borough should make trips there both easy and cheap (provided they are all finished on time, that is). Greenwich is set to join the sprawling Underground network, connecting to central London via the Jubilee line with a new station at North Greenwich, on the Greenwich peninsula. The Docklands train is being extended with a tunnel under the river, coming up to a station at Cutty Sark Gardens and one at Greenwich Railway station. Most people will journey to the Dome via the Millennium Transit Link, a shuttle service that leaves Charlton railway station. Note that the Millennium site itself is car-free. You can also get to Greenwich by riverboat from Westminster and Tower Bridge piers and by ThamesLine's high-speed river buses.

Sights to See

GREENWICH

Numbers in the text correspond to numbers in the margin and on the Greenwich.

②   **Cutty Sark.** This romantic tea clipper was built in 1869, one of fleets and fleets of similar wooden tall-masted clippers that during the 19th century plied the seven seas, trading in exotic commodities—tea, in this case. The *Cutty Sark*, the last to survive, was also the fastest, sailing the China–London route in 1871 in only 107 days. Now the photogenic vessel lies in dry dock, a museum of one kind of seafaring life—and not a comfortable kind for the 28-strong crew, as you'll see. The collection of figureheads is amusing, too. ⊠ *King William Walk,* ☎ *020/8858–3445.* 🎟 *£3.50.* 🕓 *Daily 10–5; last admission 30 mins before closing.*

①   **Millennium Dome.** Located on the Prime Meridian, or Longitude Zero, in Greenwich, the Millennium Dome is probably Europe's biggest monument to the advent of the new century. Conceived of as "a 21st-century Stonehenge" by its visionary architect Richard Rogers—who found fame and notoriety when he designed the Lloyd's of London headquarters building (☞ *above*)—and looking like a futuristic sports arena, this colossus is more than 2½ mi in circumference, with a roof 1 mi high and strong enough to support a jumbo jet. You could fit the Eiffel Tower on its side into the Dome, or even one of the Great Pyramids of Egypt. Yet while its size has always been much vaunted, its contents have been less so—up until mid-1999, the interior was a deadly secret, because, some said, the organizers did not know themselves. Until the opening ceremony on December 31,

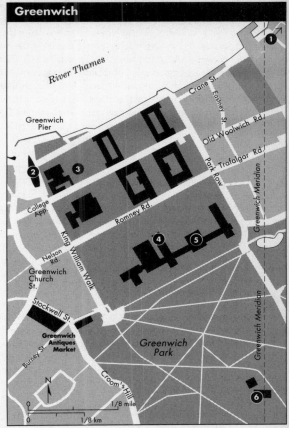

Greenwich

Cutty Sark, **2**
Millennium Dome, **1**
National Maritime Museum, **4**

Old Royal Observatory, **6**
Queen's House, **5**
Royal Naval College, **3**

1999, the great marquee will be closed to the public. After that, the doors will be thrust aside to show the 14 themed Disneylandish zones, including Work—a look at how this most central of life's activities is forever changing our lives; Learn—showing the classrooms of the future and presenting the challenges facing education; and Serious Play—an exhibition focusing on leisure. The special effects in this zone promise to be particularly spectacular and also interactive: visitors can don a Spiderman suit that sticks to the wall to climb down, having first ascended on high via a moving platform that takes them toward huge multimedia displays. Of all the exhibitions, the Body Zone is the most talked about, thanks to its larger-than-the-Statue-of-Liberty representation of the human body, which will allow visitors to journey through myriad passageways to see how our bodies function. While the emphasis is on technology and the achievements of mankind, there are zones that recognize the more spiritual side of existence: the Dreamscape zone stresses the need to relax and to let the imagination run riot with the senses. Here, you will take a seat in a boat designed as 16-seater beds and float along a "river of dreams." One may need this form of relaxation during a busy visit to the Dome, for if organizers have predicted correctly the number of visitors (35,000 to 55,000 per day), then a moment of quiet may be no bad thing. Finally, if you want to dazzle your eyes, head for the central zone, a performance area where a cast of 200 performers will put on a show with acrobatics, music, and visual effects, up to six times a day. As a look into the 21st century and what awaits us, the Millennium Dome promises much, but before its doors opened grumblings had been loud and constant from the press—in its recounting of the achievements of humanity, it makes no mention of either Shakespeare or religion, just two of many startling omissions. And groans have also arisen over the planned sales of tickets: at press time, it was announced you will not be able to buy tickets for admission on site. Instead they will be available anywhere you can buy a National Lottery ticket, via a direct ticket hot line, from train but not Underground stations, through some coach operators, and from the Web site, www.dome2000.co.uk. During most of the year, tickets will be for a one-day-long session; during the peak summer season and holidays, days will be split into two sessions. To walk to the Dome from center Greenwich and the famous Royal Naval College and Cutty Sark complex, head northeast along the Thames using the new Riverside Walk. All in all, the Dome promises to be a spectacular extravaganza, but whether or not it rivals the impact of Prince Albert's 1851 epoch-making Great Exhibition at the Crystal Palace remains to be seen. ⊠ *Millenium Dome, Drawdock St., Greenwich Peninsula,* ☎ *Public information hot line 0870/603–2000.* 🎫 *£20.* ☉ *Daily 10–6:30, peak summer months and holidays 9:30–11.*

👆 **❹ National Maritime Museum.** One of Greenwich's star attractions contains everything to do with the British at sea, in the form of paintings, models, maps, globes, sextants, uniforms (including the one Nelson died in at Trafalgar, complete with bloodstained bullet hole), and—best of all—actual boats, including a collection of ornately gilded royal barges. The museum's Dolphin Coffee Shop is a good place to recuperate after the rigors of the museum. ⊠ *Romney Rd.,* ☎ *020/8858–4422.* 🎫 *£5, including the Queen's House and Old Royal Observatory; White Card accepted.* ☉ *Mon.–Sat. 10–6, Sun. noon–6.*

❻ Old Royal Observatory. Founded in 1675 by Charles II, this observatory was designed the same year by Christopher Wren for John Flamsteed, the first Astronomer Royal. The red ball you see on its roof has been there only since 1833. It drops every day at 1 PM, and you can set your watch by it, as the sailors on the Thames always have. Everyone comes here to be photographed astride the **Prime Meridian,** a brass line laid on the cobblestones at zero degrees longitude, one side being the eastern, one the western, hemisphere. ⊠ *Greenwich Park,* ☎ *020/8858–4422.* 🎫 *£5.50, including National Maritime Museum and Queen's House; White Card accepted.* ☉ *Mon.–Sat. 10–6, Sun. noon–6.*

★ **❺ Queen's House.** The queen for whom Inigo Jones began designing the house in 1616 was James I's Anne of Denmark, but she died three years later, and it was Charles I's French wife, Henrietta Maria, who inherited the building when it was completed in 1635. It is Britain's first Classical building—the first, that is, to use the lessons of Italian Renaissance architecture—and is of enormous importance in the history of English architecture. The Great Hall is a perfect cube, exactly 40 ft in all three directions, and it is decorated with paintings of the Muses, the Virtues, and the Liberal Arts. ✉ *Romney Rd.,* ☎ *020/8858–4422.* 🎟 *£5.50, including National Maritime Museum and Old Royal Observatory; White Card accepted.* ◷ *Mon.–Sat. 10–6, Sun. noon–6.*

❸ **Royal Naval College.** Begun by Christopher Wren in 1694 as a home for ancient mariners, it became a school for young ones in 1873. You'll notice how the blocks part to reveal the **Queen's House** across the central lawns—one of England's most famous architectural set pieces. Wren, with the help of his assistant, Hawksmoor, was at pains to preserve the river vista from the house, and there are few more majestic views in London than the awe-inspiring symmetry he achieved. The Painted Hall and the College Chapel are the two outstanding interiors on view here. ✉ *King William Walk,* ☎ *020/8858–2154.* 🎟 *Free.* ◷ *Daily 2:30–4:45.*

HAMPTON COURT PALACE

Some 20 mi from central London, on a loop of the Thames upstream from Richmond, lies **Hampton Court,** one of London's oldest royal palaces, more like a small town in size, and requiring a day of your time to do it justice. The magnificent Tudor brick house was begun in 1514 by Cardinal Wolsey, the ambitious and worldly lord chancellor (roughly, prime minister) of England and archbishop of York. He wanted it to be the absolute best palace in the land, and in this he succeeded so effectively that Henry VIII grew deeply envious, whereupon Wolsey felt obliged to give Hampton Court to the king. Henry moved in in 1525, adding a great hall and chapel, and proceeded to live much of his astonishing life here. Later, during the reign of William and Mary, the palace was much expanded by Sir Christopher Wren. The site beside the slow-moving Thames is perfect. The palace itself, steeped in history, hung with priceless paintings, full of echoing cobbled courtyards and cavernous Tudor kitchens complete with deer pies and cooking pots—not to mention the ghost of Catherine Howard, who is still aboard, screaming her innocence (of adultery) to an unheeding Henry VIII—is set in a fantastic array of ornamental gardens (including a wondrous topiary maze), lakes, and ponds, which must be seen on a sunny day. ⊠ *East Mole-sey,* ☎ *020/8977–8441.* ✉ *Apartments and maze £10, maze alone £2.30, grounds free.* ⊙ *State apartments Apr.–Oct., Tues.–Sun. 9:30–6, Mon. 10:15–6; Nov.–Mar., Tues.–Sun. 9:30–4:30, Mon. 10:15–4:30; grounds daily 8–dusk.*

KEW

The **Royal Botanic Gardens** at Kew are the headquarters of the country's leading botanical institute as well as a public garden of 300 acres and more than 60,000 species of plants. Two 18th-century royal ladies, Queen Caroline and Princess Augusta, were responsible for its founding. The highlights here are the 19th-century greenhouses and the ultramodern Princess of Wales Conservatory, opened in 1987. Kew Palace, on the grounds, was home to George III for much of his life; note that the palace is closed for renovations until early 2000; call for news of its often de-layed reopening. Its formal garden is being redeveloped on a 17th-century pattern. ☎ *020/8940–1171.* ✉ *Gardens £4.50, including Queen Charlotte's Cottage (Apr.–Sept.).* ⊙ *Gardens daily 9:30–6:30, greenhouses 10–6:30 (Sun. and national holidays until 8); in winter, closing times depend on the light.*

3 Dining

NO LONGER WOULD Somerset Maugham be justified in saying, "If you want to eat well in England, have breakfast three times a day." London is in the midst of a restaurant revolution and its dining scene is one of the hottest around; even Andrew Lloyd Webber, that obsessional front-runner and composer of *Cats* and *Phantom,* has taken on a second career as dining critic. The city has fallen head-over-heels in love with its restaurants—all 5,000 of them—from its vast, glamorous eateries to its tiny neighborhood joints, from pubs where young foodniks find their feet to swanky boîtes where celebrity chefs launch their ego flights.

This restaurant renaissance is due to a talented bunch of entrepreneurs, chefs, and culinary peacocks: Sir Terence Conran, Antony Worrall Thompson, Marco Pierre White, Jean-Christophe Novelli, Oliver Peyton, Mogens Tholstrup, Christopher Corbin, and Jeremy King lead the list. Read all about them, and many others, when you get here—which you can easily do by picking up any newspaper. To keep up with the onslaught, they have about 15 restaurant reviewers apiece. Luckily, London also does a good job of catering to people more interested in satisfying their appetites without breaking the bank than in the latest food fashions. We have tried to strike a balance in our listings between these extremes, and have included hip and happening places, neighborhood places, ethnic alternatives and old favorites, plus some completely undemanding burger joints and regular restaurants for when you merely want to be fed. Ethnic restaurants have always been a good bet here, especially the thousands of Indian restaurants, since Londoners see a good tandoori as their birthright.

Few places these days mind if you order a second appetizer instead of an entrée, and you will often find set-price menus at lunchtime, bringing even the very finest and fanciest establishments within reach. Prix-fixe dinners are beginning to proliferate, too. Note that many places are closed on Sunday or late at night, and virtually everywhere closes down for the Christmas holiday period. The law obliges all British restaurants to display their prices, including VAT (sales

tax) outside, but watch for hidden extras such as bread and
vegetables charged separately, and service. Most restaurants
add 10%–15% automatically to the check, or stamp SER-
VICE NOT INCLUDED along the bottom, and/or leave the total
on the credit-card slip blank. Beware of paying twice for
service, especially if it was less than satisfactory.

CATEGORY	COST*
££££	over £50
£££	£35–£50
££	£20–£35
£	under £20

*per person, including first course, main course, and dessert,
excluding drinks, service, and VAT*

St. James's

££££ ✕ **The Ritz.** Constantly accused of being London's prettiest dining room, this palace of marble, gilt, and trompe l'oeil
would moisten even Marie Antoinette's eye; add the view
over Green Park and the Ritz's secret sunken garden, and
it seems obsolete to consider eating. But Giles Thompson's
British/French cuisine stands up to the visual onslaught
with costly morsels (foie gras, lobster, truffles, caviar, etc.),
super-rich, all served with a flourish. Englishness is wrested
from Louis XVI by a daily roast "from the trolley," or braised
oxtail, among other delicacies. A three-course prix-fixe
lunch at £34 and a dinner at £49 make the check more bear-
able, but the wine list is pricey. A Friday and Saturday dinner dance at £55 sweetly maintains a dying tradition. ⊠
Piccadilly, W1, ☎ *020/7493–8181. Reservations essential.
Jacket and tie. AE, DC, MC, V. Tube: Green Park.*

£££ ✕ **Le Caprice.** Secreted on a small street behind the Ritz,
★   Caprice may command the deepest loyalty of any London
restaurant, because it gets everything right: the glamorous,
glossy black Eva Jiricna interior, the perfect pitch of the informal but respectful service, the food, halfway between
Euro-peasant and fashion-plate. This food—crispy duck and
watercress salad; seared scallops with bacon and sorrel; Lin-
colnshire sausage with bubble and squeak (potato-and-
cabbage hash); grilled rabbit with black-olive polenta; and
divine desserts, too—has no business being so good, because

the other reason everyone comes here is that everyone else does, which leads to the best people-watching in town (apart from its almost chicer sister restaurant, The Ivy; ☞ Covent Garden, *below*). ⊠ *Arlington House, Arlington St., SW1,* ☎ *020/7629–2239. AE, DC, MC, V. No dinner Sun. Tube: Green Park.*

£££ ✕ **Quaglino's.** Now well into its first decade, Sir Terence Conran's original huge restaurant, "Quags," is *the* out-of-towners' post-theater or celebration destination, while Londoners like its late hours. The gigantic sunken restaurant boasts a glamorous staircase, "Crustacea Altar," large bar, and live jazz music. The food is fashionably pan-European with some Oriental trimmings. Desserts come from somewhere between the Paris bistro and the English nursery (raspberry sablé, crème pudding with butterscotch sauce), and wine from the Old World and the New, some bottles at modest prices. ⊠ *16 Bury St., SW1,* ☎ *020/7930–6767. AE, DC, MC, V. Tube: Green Park.*

£ ✕ **The Fountain.** At the back of Fortnum & Mason's is this
★ old-fashioned restaurant, frumpy and popular as a boarding school matron, serving delicious light meals, toasted snacks, sandwiches, and ice-cream sodas. During the day, go for the Welsh rarebit or cold game pie; in the evening, a no-frills fillet steak is a typical option. It's just the place for afternoon tea and ice-cream sundaes after the Royal Academy or Bond Street shopping, and for pre-theater meals. ⊠ *181 Piccadilly, W1,* ☎ *020/7734–4938. AE, DC, MC, V. Closed Sun. Tube: Green Park.*

Mayfair

££££ ✕ **Chez Nico at Ninety Park Lane.** Those with refined palates and very deep pockets would be well advised not to miss Nico Ladenis's exquisite cuisine, served in this suitably hushed and plush Louis XV dining room next to the Grosvenor House Hotel. Autodidact Nico is one of the world's great chefs, and he's famous for knowing it. The menu is in French and untranslated. There is no salt on the table—ask for some at your peril. It's all more affordable in daylight, proffering set menus from £34 for three courses. (For a cheaper version, the Simply Nico diffusion line of restaurants is reliably good.) ⊠ *90 Park La., W1,*

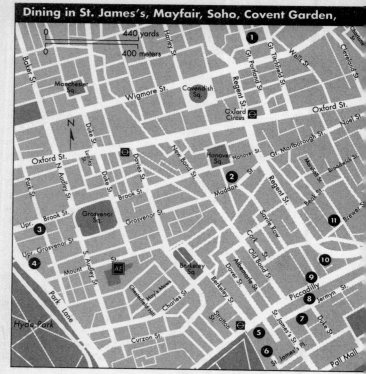

Dining in St. James's, Mayfair, Soho, Covent Garden,

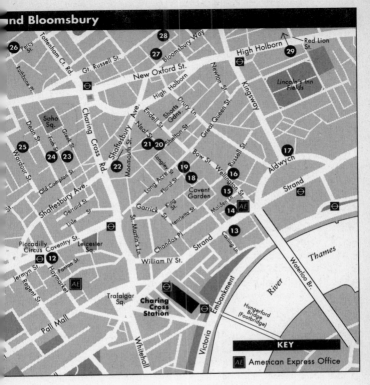

The Ritz, **5**
Rules, **15**
Savoy Grill, **13**
Soho Soho, **23**
Titanic, **11**
Truckles of Pied
Bull Yard, **28**
Villandry, **1**

☏ 020/7409–1290. *Reservations essential. Jacket and tie. AE, DC, MC, V. Closed weekends, 3 wks in Aug. Tube: Marble Arch.*

££££ ✗ **Le Gavroche.** Albert Roux has handed the toque to his son, Michel, who retains many of his capital-C Classic dishes under the heading *Hommage à mon père,* as well as adding his own style to the place that was once considered London's finest restaurant. Much of the food is still fabulous—the lobster tajine is a wonder—but the decor of the basement dining room is, some would say, generic: brown-green walls, dullish modern oil paintings, and potted plants. The set lunch is relatively affordable at £40. ✉ *43 Upper Brook St., W1,* ☏ *020/7499–1826. Reservations essential at least 1 wk in advance. Jacket and tie. AE, DC, MC, V. Closed weekends, 10 days at Christmas. Tube: Marble Arch.*

££££ ✗ **Oak Room.** Bad boy Marco Pierre White enjoys Jaggerlike
★   fame from his TV appearances and gossip column reports of his complicated love life and random eruptions of fury. He should stick to his pans, say super-chef critics, meaning it literally in some cases. But, hype aside, Marco may be London's greatest chef and now gets to show off in his most spectacular setting yet—all belle epoque soaring ceilings and gilded bits, and palms and paintings. ✉ *Le Meridien, 21 Piccadilly, W1,* ☏ *020/7437–0202. Reservations essential. Jacket and tie. AE, DC, MC, V. Tube: Piccadilly Circus.*

£££ ✗ **Criterion.** This palatial neo-Byzantine mirrored marble hall, which first opened in 1874, was put back on the map with the arrival of the current regime led by the superlative Marco Pierre White, although he doesn't perform his art here. The glamor of the soaring golden ceiling, peacock-blue theater-size drapes, oil paintings, and attentive Gallic service adds up to an elegant night out. The vast menu is difficult to ride herd on—it extends from brasserie to luxe—but the kitchen is a serious one. ✉ *Piccadilly Circus, W1,* ☏ *020/7930–2626. AE, DC, MC, V. Tube: Piccadilly Circus.*

££ ✗ **Gourmet Pizza Company.** Fine pies with wacky toppings are served up at this California-style über-pizzeria. ✉ *7–9 Swallow St., SW1,* ☏ *020/7734–5182. AE, MC, V. Tube: Piccadilly Circus.*

£–££ ✕ **Brown's.** Unpretentious, crowd-pleasing, child-friendly English food is accomplished here at the former establishment of Messrs. Cooling and Wells, the famous tailors, now converted to Edwardian style by the owner of the very successful regional Brown's (the Oxford and Cambridge ones have put generations of students through school). Eat steak and Guinness pie or salmon cakes, then sticky toffee pudding or sherry trifle. ⊠ *47 Maddox St., W1,* ☎ *020/7491–4565. AE, MC, V. Tube: Oxford Circus.*

£–££ ✕ **Villandry.** This foodie's paradise just moved to huge new premises—the food hall here is now even larger than the one at Harrods! French pâtés, Continental cheeses, fruit tarts, biscuits, and breads galore are for sale, and if you must indulge but can't wait to take a bite, there's a tearoom café and dining room that both serve exquisite lunches. Breakfast, lunch, and dinner are served daily. ⊠ *170 Great Portland St., W1,* ☎ *020/7631–3131. AE, MC, V. Tube: Great Portland St.*

Soho

£££ ✕ **Alastair Little.** Little is one of London's most original—and most imitated—chefs, drawing inspiration from practically everywhere—Thailand, Japan, Scandinavia, France, but chiefly Italy, and sometimes bringing it off brilliantly. His restaurant is stark and sparse—it's intentional, darling—so all attention focuses on the menu, which changes not once but twice daily to take advantage of the best ingredients. Look out also for his newer, smaller, cheaper version near Ladbroke Grove tube station. ⊠ *49 Frith St., W1,* ☎ *020/7734–5183. AE, DC, MC, V. Closed Sun. No lunch Sat. Tube: Leicester Sq.*

££–£££ ✕ **Titanic.** London's splashiest new restaurant is now riding high on the crest of a media wave, yet Marco Pierre White, the noted chef who opened this—the latest and greatest in the tide of trend-driven dining spots—claims it was not inspired by the blockbuster film. But like the movie, this place has pulled in the crowds, plus a clientele of the young, loud, and fashionable (Peter O'Toole, the Marquess of Londonderry). Decor is art deco ocean liner, dinner is fun and casual, ranging from fish-and-chips to squid ink risotto to sticky toffee, and prices are lower than you'd

expect for this corner of town. ⊠ *81 Brewer St., W1,* ☎
020/7437–1912. Reservations essential. AE, MC, V. Tube:
Piccadilly.

£–£££ ✕ **Mezzo.** Sir Terence Conran's gargantuan 700-seater is
not as polished as the new Sartoria, in Savile Row, or effi-
cient as Zinc, in Heddon St., but it's still funky, and the young
office and evening crowd like to hang out here. Downstairs
is the restaurant proper, with its huge glass-walled show
kitchen, its Allen Jones murals, its grand piano and dance
floor, and its typically Conran-French menu of things such
as seafood, rabbit stew, steak-frites, and fig tart. Upstairs,
the bar overlooks a canteen-style operation called Mezzo-
nine. A late-night café/patisserie/newsstand has a separate
entrance next door (and much lower prices). The place became a London landmark from day one, with much bus-
tle, despite its low celebrity count. ⊠ *100 Wardour St., W1,*
☎ *020/7314–4000. AE, DC, MC, V. Tube: Leicester Sq.*

££   ✕ **Soho Soho.** The ground floor is a lively café-bar with a
(no reservations) rotisserie, while upstairs is a more formal
and expensive restaurant. Inspiration comes from Provence,
both in the olive-oil cooking style and the decor, with its murals, primary colors, and pale ocher terra-cotta floor tiles.
The rotisserie serves omelets, salads, charcuterie, and cheeses,
plus a handful of such bistro dishes as Toulouse sausages with
fries; herbed, grilled sole; and tarte Tatin. Or you can stay
in the café-bar and have just a Kir or a beer. ⊠ *11–13 Frith
St., W1,* ☎ *020/7494–3491. Reservations essential. AE,
DC, MC, V. Sun. brasserie open only. Tube: Leicester Sq.*

Covent Garden

££££ ✕ **Savoy Grill.** The grill continues in the first rank of power
dining locations. Politicians, newspaper barons, and tycoons
like the comforting food and impeccably discreet and attentive service in the low-key, yew-panel salon. On the
menu, an omelet Arnold Bennett (with cheese and smoked
fish) is perennial, as are beef Wellington on Tuesday and
roast Norfolk duck on Friday. Play goers can split their theater menu, eating part of their meal before the show, the
rest after. Diners can also get their dancing shoes on at the
weekly "Stompin' at the Savoy" events. ⊠ *The Strand, WC2,*

☎ *020/7836–4343. Reservations essential. Jacket and tie. AE, DC, MC, V. Closed Sun. No lunch Sat. Tube: Aldwych.*

£££ ✕ **The Ivy.** This seems to be everybody's favorite restaurant—
★ everybody who works in the media or the arts, that is. In a Deco dining room with blinding white tablecloths, and Hodgkins and Paolozzis on the walls, the celebrated and the wanna-bes eat Caesar salad, roast grouse, shrimp gumbo, braised oxtail, and rice pudding with Armagnac prunes, or sticky toffee pudding. ⊠ *1 West St., WC2,* ☎ *020/7836–4751. Reservations essential. AE, DC, MC, V. Tube: Covent Garden.*

£££ ✕ **Orso.** The Italian brother of Joe Allen (☞ *below*), this basement restaurant has the same snappy staff and a glitzy clientele of showbiz types and hacks. The Tuscan-style menu changes every day but always includes excellent pizza and pasta dishes. Food here, much like the place itself, is never boring. Orsino, in W11, is a stylish offshoot, serving much the same fare. ⊠ *27 Wellington St., WC2,* ☎ *020/ 7240–5269. AE, MC, V. Tube: Covent Garden.*

£££ ✕ **Rules.** Come, take an escape from the 20th century. Al-
★ most 200 years old, this London institution has welcomed everyone from Dickens to Charlie Chaplin to Lillie Langtry, who used to come here with the Prince of Wales. The menu is historic and good—try its fabled steak and kidney and mushroom pudding for a virtual taste of the 18th century—but the decor is even more delicious. With plush red banquettes and lacquered Victorian-yellow walls, which are festively adorned with 19th-century oil paintings and hundreds of engravings, this is probably the most handsome dining salon in London (note, however, that this restaurant has three floors). It is more than a little touristy, but that's because it's so quaint. ⊠ *35 Maiden La., WC2,* ☎ *020/ 7836–5314. Reservations essential. AE, DC, MC, V. Tube: Covent Garden.*

££ ✕ **Bank.** City and fashionable folk flock to this vast eatery
★ with its spectacular chandelier and equally exciting menu. Seared fish and blackened chicken, pak-choi and puy lentils; mousses, brûlées, and nursery puds, are just small examples of the fast-changing, world palette, with a definitive Mod-Brit touch. While not a steal price-wise, the dishes rarely fail to please. ⊠ *1 Kingsway, WC2,* ☎ *020/7379–9797.*

Reservations essential. AE, DC, MC, V. Tube: Covent Garden, Holborn.

££ ✕ **Bertorelli's.** Right across from the stage door of the Royal Opera House, Bertorelli's is quietly chic, the food tempting and just innovative enough: poached cotechino sausage with lentils or monkfish ragout with fennel, tomato, and olives are typical dishes. A recent complete overhaul has brought the decor into a new era. Even more brilliant cuisine and decorous ambience can be found at the branch on Charlotte St. ✉ *44A Floral St., WC2,* ☎ *020/7836–3969. AE, DC, MC, V. Tube: Covent Garden.*

££ ✕ **Joe Allen.** Long hours (thespians flock here after the curtain falls in Theatreland) and a welcoming, if loud, brick-wall interior mean New York Joe's London branch is still swinging after two decades. The fun, California-inflected menu helps. It can get chaotic, with long waits for the cute waiters, but at least there will be famous faces to ogle in the meantime. The brunch, served Sunday, noon–4, is one of London's most convivial. ✉ *13 Exeter St., WC2,* ☎ *020/7836–0651. Reservations essential. AE, MC, V. Tube: Covent Garden.*

£–££ ✕ **Belgo Centraal.** The wackiest dining concept in town started with a bistro in Camden, and was so adored it was cloned uptown in a big basement space you have to enter by elevator. Have mussels and fries in vast quantity, served with 100 Belgian beers (fruit-flavored, Trappist-brewed, white, or light) by people dressed as monks in a hall like a refectory in a Martian monastery. The luxury index may be low, but so is the check. ✉ *50 Earlham St., WC2,* ☎ *020/7813–2233. AE, DC, MC, V. Tube: Covent Garden.*

£ ✕ **Food for Thought.** This simple basement restaurant (no liquor license) seats only 50 and is extremely popular, so you'll almost always find a line of people down the stairs. The menu—stir-fries, casseroles, salads, and desserts—changes every day, and each dish is freshly made; there's no microwave. ✉ *31 Neal St., WC2,* ☎ *020/7836–0239. Reservations not accepted. No credit cards. Closed after 8 pm, 2 wks at Christmas. Tube: Covent Garden.*

£ ✕ **Maxwell's.** London's first-ever burger joint, which turned 25 in '97, cloned itself and then grew up. Here's the result, a happy place under the Opera House serving the kind of food you're homesick for: quesadillas and nachos, Buffalo chicken wings, barbecue ribs, Cajun chicken, chef's salad, a real NYC Reuben, and a burger to die for. ⊠ *8–9 James St., WC2,* ☎ *020/7836–0303. AE, DC, V. Tube: Covent Garden.*

Bloomsbury

££ ✕ **Chez Gérard.** One of a small chain of steak-frites restaurants, this one has expanded its utterly Gallic menu to include more for non–red meat eaters. Steak, served with shoestring fries and béarnaise sauce, remains the reason to visit. ⊠ *8 Charlotte St., W1,* ☎ *020/7636–4975. AE, DC, MC, V. Tube: Goodge St.*

££ ✕ **Museum Street Café.** This useful and reliable restaurant near the British Museum serves a limited selection of impeccably fresh dishes, intelligently and plainly cooked by the two young owners, and charged prix-fixe. The evening menu might feature char-grilled, maize-fed chicken with pesto, followed by a rich chocolate cake; at lunchtime you might choose a sandwich of Stilton on walnut bread and a big bowl of soup. The place is now open for breakfast at 8 AM (9 on Saturday) and serving a home-baked and wholesome tea (3 PM Saturday only). There is an atypical (for London) ban on smoking. ⊠ *47 Museum St., WC1,* ☎ *020/ 7405–3211. Reservations essential. AE, MC, V. Closed Sun. Tube: Tottenham Court Rd.*

£ ✕ **North Sea Fish Restaurant.** This is the place for the British national dish of fish-and-chips—battered and deep-fried whitefish with thick fries shaken with salt and vinegar. It's a bit tricky to find—three blocks south of St. Pancras station, down Judd Street. Only freshly caught fish is served, and you can order it grilled—though that would defeat the purpose. You can take your meals out in true grab-and-gulp fashion or eat in. ⊠ *7–8 Leigh St., WC1,* ☎ *020/7387–5892. AE, DC, MC, V. Closed Sun. Tube: Russell Sq.*

£ ✕ **Truckles of Pied Bull Yard.** Wine bars were the hits of '70s London, though hardly any survive to tell the tale. This one's fantastic for a post–British Museum glass of something—and they purportedly serve the cheapest glass of bubbly here. The old English ham salad has gone upscale, and southern European foods (ciabatta sandwich with goat's cheese) are

more often than not on the menu. The nicest area is the court-
yard with tables galore in summer. ⊠ *Off Bury Place,
WC1,* ☎ *020/7404–5338, AE, DC, MC, V. Closed Sun.
No dinner Sat. Tube: Holborn.*

Knightsbridge and South Kensington

££££   ✕ **The Capital.** This elegant, clublike dining room has chandeliers and greige rag-rolled walls, a grown-up atmosphere,
and formal service. Chef Philip Britten's fusion French/Ital-
ian/Asian never fails to astonish. Meats are cooked in carefully selected aromatic whole spices or toasted nuts, and
infused with wine. Desserts follow the same exciting route.
Set-price menus at lunch (£28) make it somewhat more affordable. ⊠ *22–24 Basil St., SW3,* ☎ *020/7589–5171.
Reservations essential. Jacket and tie. AE, DC, MC, V.
Tube: Knightsbridge.*

££££   ✕ **La Tante Claire.** One of the best restaurants in London
  ★   has upped its sticks, pots, and pans and moved to the
Berkeley Hotel. Chef Pierre Koffmann still reigns over the
kitchen, so you can expect the same blindingly brilliant standards of haute cuisine. From the *carte,* you might choose
hot pâté de foie gras on shredded potatoes with a sweet wine
and shallot sauce, roast spiced pigeon, or Koffmann's signature dish of pigs' feet stuffed with mousse of white meat
with sweetbreads and wild mushrooms. The set lunch menu
is a genuine bargain. Lunch reservations must be made 2–
3 days in advance, dinner reservations 3–4 weeks in advance.
⊠ *Berkeley Hotel, Wilton Place, SW1,* ☎ *020/7823–2003.
Reservations essential. Jacket and tie. AE, DC, MC, V.
Closed weekends. Tube: Knightsbridge.*

£££   ✕ **Zafferano.** Princess Margaret, Eric Clapton, Joan Collins,
  ★   and any number of Cartier-brooch-wearing neighborhood
Belgravians have flocked to this place, which, since 1995,
has been London's best exponent of *cucina nuova.* The fireworks are in the kitchen, not in the brick-wall-and-saffron-
hued decor, but *what* fireworks: pumpkin ravioli with a
splash of Amaretto, *mondeghini ai crostini di risotto* (minced
pork wrapped in Savoy cabbage leaves), and monkfish
with walnuts. The desserts are also *delizioso,* especially the
Sardinian pecorino pastries served with undersweetened
vanilla ice cream. Be sure to book early. ⊠ *15 Lowndes*

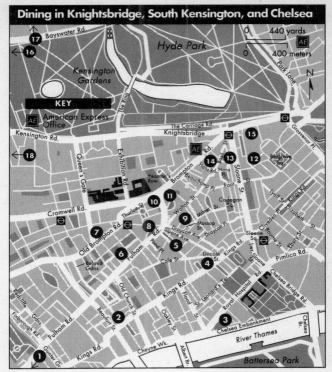

Dining in Knightsbridge, South Kensington, and Chelsea

Bibendum, **5**

Bluebird, **2**

Brasserie St.
Quentin, **11**

Cactus Blue, **6**

The Capital, **14**

Chelsea
Kitchen, **4**

Chutney Mary, **1**

The
Collection, **10**

The Cow, **17**

The
Enterprise, **9**

Gordon
Ramsay, **3**

Pasha, **7**

Pharmacy, **16**

PJ's, **8**

Stockpot, **13**

Wódka, **18**

La Tante
Claire, **15**

Zafferano, **12**

St., SW1, ☎ 020/7235–5800. Reservations essential. AE, MC, V. Tube: Knightsbridge.

££ ✕ **Brasserie St. Quentin.** A very popular slice of Paris, this is a popular spot frequented by French expatriates and locals alike. Every inch of the Gallic menu is explored—quiche, escargots, cassoulet, lemon tart—in the bourgeois provincial comfort so many London bistro chains try for yet fail to achieve. ⊠ *243 Brompton Rd., SW3, ☎ 020/7589–8005. AE, DC, MC, V. Tube: South Kensington.*

£–££ ✕ **The Enterprise.** One of the new luxury breed of "gastro-pubs," this is perhaps the chicest of the lot—near Harrods and Brompton Cross, it's filled with decorative types who complement the decor: paisley-stripe wallpaper, Edwardian side tables covered with baskets and farmhouse fruit, vintage books piled up in the windows, white linen and fresh flowers on the tables. The menu isn't overly pretty—char-grilled squid stuffed with almonds, entrecôte steak, salmon with artichoke hearts—but the ambience certainly is. ⊠ *35 Walton St., SW3, ☎ 020/7584–3148. AE, MC, V. Tube: South Kensington.*

£ ✕ **Stockpot.** You'll find speedy service in this large, jolly restaurant packed with young people and shoppers. The food is filling and wholesome, in a Lancashire-hot-pot, spaghetti-Bolognese, apple-crumble way. ⊠ *6 Basil St., SW3, ☎ 020/7589–8627. No credit cards. Tube: Knightsbridge. Other branches: ⊠ 40 Panton St., off Leicester Sq., ☎ 020/7839–5142; ⊠ 18 Old Compton St., Soho, ☎ 020/7287–1066; and ⊠ 273 King's Rd., Chelsea, ☎ 020/7823–3175.*

Chelsea

£££– ✕ **Gordon Ramsay.** A table at Ramsay's restaurant has
££££ been London's toughest reservation to score for almost as long as it's been open, because the soccer star-turned-chef has every table gasping in awe at his famous witty cappuccino of white beans with sautéed girolles and truffles, followed by—well, anything at all. Reserve months ahead; go for lunch (£24) if money is an object. *68-69 Royal Hospital Rd., SW3, ☎ 020/7352–4441/3334. Reservations essential. AE, DC, MC, V. Closed weekends. Tube: Sloane Square.*

£££ ✗ **Chutney Mary.** London's first-and-only Anglo-Indian restaurant provides a fantasy version of the British Raj, all giant wicker armchairs and palms. Dishes like Masala roast lamb (practically a whole leg, marinated and spiced) and "Country Captain" (braised chicken with almonds, raisins, chilies, and spices) alternate with the more familiar North Indian dishes such as *roghan josh* (lamb curry). The best choices are certainly the dishes re-created from the kitchens of Indian chefs cooking for English palates back in the old Raj days. ✉ *535 King's Rd., SW10,* ☎ *020/7351–3113. AE, DC, MC, V. Tube: Fulham Broadway.*

£££ ✗ **The Collection.** Enter the former Katharine Hamnett shop through the spotlighted tunnel over the glass draw-bridge to find a vast warehouse setting—adorned with in-dustrial wooden beams and steel cables, a huge bar, and a suspended gallery, it seems more dance club than eatery. Around you is the local ab-fab crowd gawking at the neigh-boring tables for an Amber Valletta sighting, or hoping owner-*doré* Mogens Tholstrup will table-hop to theirs, while they pick at Med food seasoned with Japanese and Thai bits and bobs (seared tuna with sesame, soy, and shi-itakes; sea bream with cilantro). Ah, fashion, fashion, fash-ion! ✉ *264 Brompton Rd.,* ☎ *020/7225–1212. AE, DC, MC, V. No dinner Sun. Tube: South Kensington.*

££–£££ ✗ **Bluebird.** Here's another Terence Conran "gastrodome"—supermarket, brasserie, fruit stand, butcher shop, bou-tique, and café-restaurant, all housed in a snappy King's Road former garage. The place is pale blue and white, very light, and not in the least cozy, with food listed in formu-lae: steamed mussels, saffron, leeks; or roasted pheasant, creamed cabbage, shallots; then chilled fruits, apple water ice. Go for the synergy and visual excitement—Conran's chefs share a tendency to promise more than they deliver. ✉ *350 King's Rd., SW3,* ☎ *020/7559–1000. Reservations essential. AE, DC, MC, V. Tube: Sloane Sq.*

££ ✗ **Cactus Blue.** Southwestern food from America is a hot thing on the London dining scene, and this place is one of a flush of new Tex-Mex spots with attitude. You can find the buzz on split levels of ochre hues, which help offset dra-matic cacti. On offer are tequilas, beers, and Baja wines, which help the crab stacks and quesadillas slide down. ✉

86 Fulham Rd., SW3, ☎ *020/7283–7858. AE, MC, V.
Tube: South Kensington.*

££ ✕ **PJ's.** The decor here evokes the Bulldog Drummond
lifestyle, with wooden floors and stained glass, a vast, slowly
revolving propeller from a 1940s Curtis flying boat, and polo
memorabilia. A menu of all-American staples should please
all but vegetarians. ✉ *52 Fulham Rd., SW3,* ☎ *020/7581–
0025. AE, DC, MC, V. Tube: South Kensington.*

£ ✕ **Chelsea Kitchen.** Always crowded, this place is fine for
hot, filling, and inexpensive food. ✉ *98 King's Rd., SW3,*
☎ *020/7589–1330. No credit cards. Tube: Sloane Sq.*

Kensington and Notting Hill Gate

££££ ✕ **Bibendum.** In the swinging '80s, this was one of Lon-
★   don's hottest places. It has cooled down now, but everyone still loves its reconditioned Michelin House setting
with its Art Deco decorations and brilliant stained glass,
Conran Shop, and Oyster Bar. Current chef Matthew Har-
ris aspires to simple but perfect dishes—herrings with sour
cream, a risotto, or leeks vinaigrette followed by steak au
poivre, or you might try brains or tripe as they ought to be
cooked. The £28 set-price menu at lunchtime is money well
spent. ✉ *Michelin House, 81 Fulham Rd., SW3,* ☎ *020/
7581–5817. Reservations essential. AE, DC, MC, V. Tube:
South Kensington.*

££ ✕ **The Cow.** Oh, no, not *another* Conran. Yes, this place
belongs to Tom, son of Sir Terrence, though it's a million
miles from Quag's and Mezzo. Actually a tiny and chic "gastro-pub," it comprises a faux-Dublin backroom bar serving up oysters, crab salad, and pasta with wine; upstairs,
a serious chef whips up Tuscan/British specialties—skate
poached in minestrone is one temptation. Notting Hillbillies and other stylish folk adore the house special—a half-
dozen Irish rock oysters with a pint of Guinness, as well
as the mixed grills and steaks that often figure on the menu.
✉ *89 Westbourne Park Rd., W2,* ☎ *020/7221–5400.
Reservations essential. MC, V. No dinner Sun. Tube: Westbourne Park.*

££ ✕ **Pasha.** Not quite a taste of old Tangiers, Pasha delivers
modern Morocco and due east in a very à la mode man-
ner. Waiters in traditional dress drift between piles of silken

cushions and flickering candlelight to bring delicacies such as *pastilla* (pie) of pigeon and stylish cross-cuisine desserts (brûlée with exotic North African fruits). ⊠ *1 Gloucester Rd., SW7,* ☎ *020/7589–7969. Reservations essential. AE, MC, V. Tube: Gloucester Rd..*

££ ✕ **Pharmacy.** London's latest scene-arena, the Pharmacy is one of those see-and-be-seen places where the bar is larger than the restaurant. In this case, the bar seats 180 and is shaped like gigantic aspirin. Yes, this place looks just like its namesake, the wait staff is garbed like hospital orderlies, and even the menu looks fab—but then Damien Hirst, artist-provocateur extraordinaire, is involved. The menu highlights "comfort food" and ranges from fisherman's pie and scrambled eggs with black truffles to spit-roast Landes duck, sauce *aigre-doux.* If you can't snag a table, just have fun at the bar—the crowd will probably be among London's trendiest. ⊠ *150 Notting Hill Gate, W11,* ☎ *020/7221–2442. AE, MC, V. Tube: Notting Hill Gate.*

££ ✕ **Wódka.** This smart, modern Polish restaurant serves the smartest, most modern Polish food around. It is popular with elegant locals plus a sprinkling of celebs and often has the atmosphere of a dinner party. With your smoked salmon, herring, caviar, eggplant *blinis,* or venison sausages, order a carafe of the purest vodka in town (and watch the check inflate); it's encased in a block of ice and hand-flavored with rowanberries. ⊠ *12 St. Albans Grove,* ☎ *020/7937–6513. Reservations essential. AE, DC, MC, V. No lunch weekends. Tube: High Street Kensington.*

City and South Bank

£££ ✕ **Le Pont de la Tour.** Sir Terence Conran's place across the
  ★   river, overlooking the bridge—that gorgeous icon, Tower Bridge—that gives it its name, comes into its own in summer, when the outside tables are heaven. Inside, there's a vintner, baker, deli, seafood bar, brasserie, and this '30s diner-style restaurant, smart as the captain's table. Fish and seafood (lobster salad; Baltic herrings in crème fraîche; roast halibut with aioli), meat and game (venison fillet, port and blueberry sauce; roast veal, caramelized endive) feature heavily—vegetarians are out of luck. Prune and Armagnac tart or chocolate terrine could finish a glamorous—and

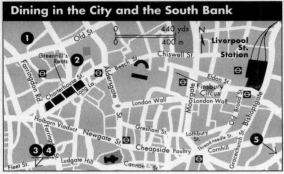

Dining in the City and the South Bank

expensive—meal. By contrast, an impeccable *salade niçoise* in the brasserie is about £9. ⊠ *36D Shad Thames, Butler's Wharf, SE1,* ☎ *020/7403–8403. Reservations essential. MC, V. Tube: Tower Hill.*

££–£££ ✕ **Maison Novelli.** Jean-Christophe Novelli is one of the
★ heroes of the Mod Brit/French cuisine, and his restaurant has drawn foodies from the day it opened in up-and-coming Clerkenwell. Richard Guest runs the kitchen as Novelli has been busy expanding his signature dishes at restaurants across town and sharing his cooking secrets in *The Times.* Guest gets the juices flowing and exploding with such favorites as confit of goose neck stuffed with fois gras, four-hour braised oxtail with licorice sauce, or the famed pig's trotter stuffed "following the mood of the day." The cheaper brasserie operation, Novelli EC1, is now next door. For very haute cuisine, try Novelli's Les Saveurs, Curzon Street in Mayfair; for cheaper and informal, the wildly popular Novelli W8, in Kensington. ⊠ *29 Clerkenwell Green, EC1,* ☎ *020/7251–6606. Reservations essential. AE, DC, MC, V. Tube: Farringdon.*

££–£££ ✕ **OXO Tower Brasserie and Restaurant.** How delightful it is for London finally to get a room with a view, and *such* a view. On the eighth floor of the Thames-side, beautifully revived, Art Deco Oxo Tower building (near the South Bank Centre) is this elegant space, featuring Euro food with this year's trendy ingredients (acorn-fed black pig charcuterie with tomato and pear chutney; calves kidneys with persillade sauce and beetroot jus; Dover sole with sea urchin butter). The ceiling slats turn and change from white to midnight blue, but who on earth notices, with St. Paul's across the water? Summertime, the terrace tables are the best places in London. ⊠ *Bankside, SE1,* ☎ *020/7803–3888. AE, MC, V. Tube: Waterloo.*

££ ✗ **People's Palace.** Thank goodness—thanks to this place, you can finally have a civilized meal during your South Bank arts encounter. With menus by trendy chef Gary Rhodes, this has remarkably low prices considering it has the greatest river view in town (apart from OXO). As the baying critics noted around opening time, there are occasional mistakes here, but the more British the dish, the more reliable it proves—suckling pig sandwich on granary bread, marmalade sponge cake, and sticky toffee pudding are good choices. ⊠ *Royal Festival Hall, Level 3, South Bank, SE1,* ☎ *020/7928–9999. AE, DC, MC, V. Tube: Waterloo.*

££ ✗ **St. John.** This former smokehouse (ham, not cigars), converted by erstwhile architect owner-chef, Fergus Henderson, has soaring white walls, schoolroom lamps, stone floors, iron railings, and plain wooden chairs. Entrées (roast lamb and parsnip, smoked haddock and fennel, deviled crab) are hearty and unadorned, but usually taste great. Service is efficiently matey. ⊠ *26 St. John St., EC1,* ☎ *020/ 7251–0848. Reservations essential. AE, MC, V. No dinner Sun. Tube: Farringdon.*

Pubs

London's pubs include some of the most gorgeous and historic interiors in London. An integral part of the British way of life, public houses dispense beer "on tap," and usually a basic, inexpensive menu of sandwiches, quiche, and salads, and other snacks at lunchtime. But you don't go to a "local" for just pub grub. Rather, pubs are the best place to get to meet the locals in their habitat. Sit at a table if you want privacy; better, help prop up the bar, where no introductions are needed, and watch that legendary British reserve fade away.

As we write, "gastro-pub" fever has hit London. At many places, chargrills are being installed in the kitchen out back, while up front the faded wallpapers and the dear ole mums are being replaced by abstract paintings and food mavens galore (the best of these new luxe pubs are reviewed above). Some of the following also feature nouveau pub grub, but whether you have Moroccan chicken or the usually dismal ploughman's special, you'll want to order a pint. Note that American-style beer is called "lager" in Britain, while the real Brit brew is "bitters." You can order up your choice in two sizes—pints or half pints (if this is your first taste of British beer, order a half). Some London pubs also sell "real ale," which is less gassy than bitters and, many would argue, has a better flavor. Remember that many pubs stop serving alcoholic beverages at 11 PM.

✕ **Black Friar.** A step from Blackfriars tube, this stunning pub has an Arts-and-Crafts interior that is entertainingly, satirically ecclesiastical, with inlaid mother-of-pearl, wood carvings, stained glass, and marble pillars all over the place, and reliefs of monks and friars poised above finely lettered temperance tracts, regardless of which there are a handful of beers on tap from independent brewers. ⊠ *174 Queen Victoria St., EC4,* ☎ *020/7236–5650.*

✕ **Dove Inn.** Read the list of famous ex-regulars, from Charles II and Nell Gwynn (mere rumor, but a likely one) to Ernest Hemingway, as you queue ages for a beer at this very popular, very comely 16th-century riverside pub by Hammersmith Bridge. If it's *too* full, stroll upstream to the Old Ship or the Blue Anchor. ⊠ *19 Upper Mall, W6,* ☎ *020/8748–5405.*

✕ **George Inn.** Sitting in a courtyard where Shakespeare's plays were once performed, the present building dates from the late 17th century and is central London's last remaining galleried inn. Dickens was a regular—the Southwark district inn is featured in *Little Dorrit.* ⊠ *77 Borough High St., SE1,* ☎ *020/7407–2056.*

✕ **Lamb and Flag.** This 17th-century pub was once known as "The Bucket of Blood," because the upstairs room was used as a ring for bare-knuckle boxing. Now, it's a trendy, friendly, and entirely bloodless pub, serving food (at lunchtime only) and real ale. It's on the edge of Covent Garden, off Garrick Street. ⊠ *33 Rose St., WC2,* ☎ *020/ 7497–9504.*

✕ **Mayflower.** An atmospheric 17th-century riverside inn in the Rotherhithe district, with exposed beams and a terrace, this is practically the very place from which the Pilgrims set sail for Plymouth Rock. The inn is licensed to sell American postage stamps. ⊠ *117 Rotherhithe St., SE16,* ☎ *020/7237–4088.*

✕ **Museum Tavern.** Across the street from the British Museum, this gloriously Victorian pub makes an ideal resting place after the rigors of the culture trail. With lots of fancy glass—etched mirrors and stained-glass panels—gilded pillars, and carvings, the heavily restored hostelry once helped Karl Marx to unwind after a hard day in the library. He could have spent his capital on any one of six beers available on tap. ⊠ *49 Great Russell St., WC1,* ☎ *020/7242–8987.*

✕ **Sherlock Holmes.** This Westminster district pub used to be known as the Northumberland Arms, and Arthur Conan Doyle popped in regularly for a pint. It figures in *The Hound of the Baskervilles,* and you can see the hound's head and plaster casts of its huge paws among other Holmes memorabilia in the bar. ⊠ *10 Northumberland St., WC2,* ☎ *020/7930–2644.*

✕ **Ye Olde Cheshire Cheese.** Yes, it is a tourist trap, but this most historic of all London pubs (it dates from 1667) deserves a visit anyway, for its sawdust-covered floors, low wood-beam ceilings, and the 14th-century crypt of a Whitefriars' monastery under the cellar bar. This was the most regular of Dr. Johnson's and Dickens's *many* locals. It's in the City. ⊠ *145 Fleet St., EC4,* ☎ *020/7353–6170.*

Afternoon Tea

In the grandest places, teatime is still a ritual, so be prepared for a dress code: Claridge's, the Ritz, and the Savoy all require jacket and tie.

✕ **Brown's Hotel.** Famous for its teas, this hotel lounge does rest on its laurels somewhat, with a packaged aura and nobody around but fellow tourists. For £17.95 you get sandwiches, a scone with cream and jam (jelly), tart, fruitcake, and shortbread. ⊠ *33 Albermarle St., W1,* ☎ *020/7518–4108. Tea served daily 3–6.*

✕ **Claridge's.** This is the real McCoy, complete with liveried footmen proffering sandwiches, a scone, and superior pastries (£18.50) in the palatial yet genteel foyer, all to the tune of the resident "Hungarian orchestra" (actually a string quartet). ✉ *Brook St., W1,* ☎ *020/7629–8860. Tea served daily 3–5.*

✗ **Fortnum & Mason's.** Upstairs at the Queen's grocer's, three set teas are ceremoniously offered: standard Afternoon Tea (sandwiches, scone, cakes, £13.50), old-fashioned high tea (the traditional nursery meal, adding something more robust and savory, £16.50), and Champagne Tea (£18.95). ✉ *St. James's Restaurant, 4th floor, 181 Piccadilly, W1,* ☎ *020/7734–8040. Tea served Mon.–Sat. 3–5:20.*

✗ **Harrods.** The Georgian Room at the ridiculously well-known department store has an afternoon tea that'll give you a sugar rush for a week. ✉ *Brompton Rd., SW3,* ☎ *020/7730–1234. Tea served Mon.–Sat. 3–5:30.*

✗ **The Ritz.** The Ritz's stagey Palm Court offers tiered cake stands, silver pots, a harpist, and Louis XVI chaises, plus a great deal of Rococo gilt and glitz, all for £22.50. It's a good excuse for a glass of champagne. Reservations are booked months in advance for weekends. ✉ *Piccadilly, W1,* ☎ *020/7493–8181. Tea served daily 2–6.*

✗ **Savoy.** The glamorous Thames-side hotel does one of the most pleasant teas, its triple-tier cake stands packed with goodies, its tailcoated waiters thrillingly polite. ✉ *The Strand, WC2,* ☎ *020/7836–4343. Tea served daily 3–5:30.*

4 Lodging

STAYING AT ONE OF LONDON'S grand-dame hotels is the next best thing—some say better—to being a guest at the palace. Royally resplendent decors abound and armies of extra-solicitous staff are stuck in the pampering mode—the Windsors should have it so good. But even in more affordable choices, classic British style brings you a taste of home, with tea-makers and Queen Mum pastel wallpapers. Still not cozy enough? Borrow some door keys, and be a B&B guest. Happily, there is no dearth of options where friendliness outdistances luxe, and we've included the best of the budget places.

We quote the average room cost as of spring 1999; in some establishments, especially those in the ££££ category, you could pay considerably more—well past the £200 mark in some cases. In any event, you should confirm *exactly* what your room costs before checking in. British hotels are obliged by law to display a price chart at the reception desk; study it carefully. In January and February you'll often find reduced rates, and large hotels with a business clientele have frequent weekend packages. The custom these days in all but the cheaper hotels is for quoted prices to cover room alone; breakfast, whether Continental or "Full English," costs extra. VAT (Value Added Tax—sales tax) is usually included, and service, too, in nearly all cases. Be sure to reserve, as special events can fill hotel rooms suddenly.

If you do manage to arrive in the capital without a room, the **London Tourist Board Information Centres** at Heathrow and Victoria Station Forecourt can help (☎ 0839/123435; calls cost 49p per minute), and the **Visitor Call** service (☎ 0891/505487) provides general advice calls cost 49p per minute); or call the **LTB Bookings Hotline** (☎ 020/7932-2020), open weekdays 9:30–5:30, for prepaid credit-card bookings (MC, V).

CATEGORY	COST*
££££	over £200
£££	£140–£200
££	£80–£140
£	under £80

All prices are for a double room; VAT included.

Mayfair, St. James's, and Victoria

££££   🏨 **Brown's.** Founded in 1837 by Lord Byron's "gentleman's gentleman," James Brown, this Victorian country house in central Mayfair occupies 11 Georgian houses and is frequented by many Anglophilic Americans—a habit that was established by the two Roosevelts (Teddy while on honeymoon). Bedrooms feature thick carpets, soft armchairs, sweeping drapes, brass chandeliers, and moiré or brocade wallpapers, as well as air-conditioning; the public rooms retain their cozy oak-panel, chintz-laden, grandfather-clock-ticking-in-the-parlor ambience. ✉ *34 Albemarle St., W1X 4BT,* ☎ *020/7493–6020,* ℻ *020/7493–9381. 118 rooms with bath. Restaurant, bar. AE, DC, MC, V. Tube: Green Park.*

££££   🏨 **Claridge's.** A hotel legend, Claridge's has one of the
★   world's classiest guest lists. The liveried staff are friendly and not in the least condescending, and the rooms are never less than luxurious—even more so now that the hotel is in the midst of a major, multimillion-dollar sprucing-up. It was founded in 1812, but the present decor is either 1930s Art Deco or country-house traditional. Have a drink in the foyer lounge with its Hungarian mini-orchestra, or retreat to the reading room for perfect quiet, interrupted only by the sound of pages turning. The bedrooms are spacious, as are the bathrooms. Beds are handmade and supremely comfortable—the King of Morocco once brought his own, couldn't sleep, and ended up ordering 30 from Claridge's to take home. ✉ *Brook St., W1A 2JQ,* ☎ *020/7629–8860 or 800/223–6800,* ℻ *020/7499–2210. 200 rooms with bath. 2 restaurants, beauty salon, exercise room. AE, DC, MC, V. Tube: Bond St.*

££££   🏨 **Connaught.** Make reservations well in advance for this
★   *very* exclusive, very British hotel just off Grosvenor Square—the most understated of any of London's grand hostelries. The bar and lounges have the air of an ambassadorial residence, an impression reinforced by the imposing oak staircase and dignified staff. Each bedroom has a foyer, antique furniture (if you don't like the desk, they'll change it), and fresh flowers, and the management is above such vulgarities as brochure and tariff—which would be extraneous for guests who inherited the Connaught habit from their

Lodging in Mayfair, St. James's, Victoria, Marylebone,

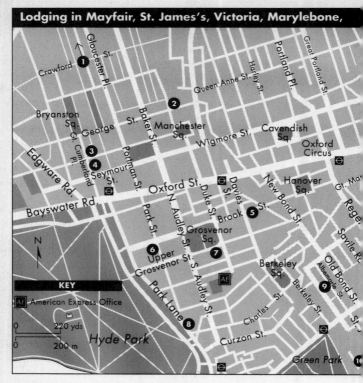

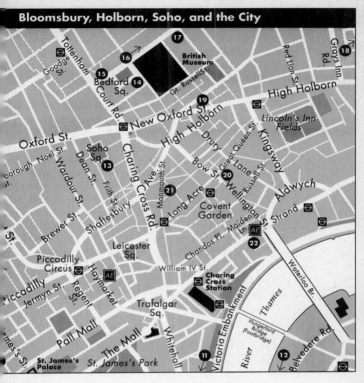

Bloomsbury, Holborn, Soho, and the City

Morgan, **14**
Myhotel, **15**
The Rookery, **18**

St. Margaret's, **17**
The Savoy, **22**
Stakis St. Ermins, **11**

great-grandfathers, anyway. If you value privacy, discretion, and the kind of luxury that eschews labels, then you have met your match here. ⊠ *Carlos Pl., W1Y 6AL,* ☎ *020/7499–7070,* ℻ *020/7495–3262. 90 rooms with bath. Restaurant, bar. MC. Tube: Bond St.*

££££   🏨 **The Dorchester.** A London institution, the Dorchester ap-
  ★   pears on every "World's Best" list. The glamour level is off the scale: 1,200 square ft of gold leaf, 800 of marble, and 2,000 of hand-tufted carpet gild this lily, and bedrooms feature Irish linen sheets on canopied beds; brocades and velvets; Italian marble and etched-glass bathrooms with Floris toiletry goodies; individual climate control; dual-voltage outlets; and cable TV. Afternoon tea, drinking, lounging, and posing are all accomplished in the catwalk-shape Promenade lounge, where you may spot one of the film-star types who will stay nowhere else. Probably no other hotel this opulent manages to be this charming. ⊠ *Park La., W1A 2HJ,* ☎ *020/7629–8888,* ℻ *020/7409–0114. 197 rooms with bath, 55 suites with bath. 3 restaurants, bar, lobby lounge, health club, nightclub, business services, meeting rooms. AE, DC, MC, V. Tube: Marble Arch.*

££££   🏨 **Grosvenor House.** "The old lady of Park Lane" is back in top-dowager position, having thrown off her creeping frumpiness during a complete overhaul. It's not the kind of place that encourages hushed whispers or that frowns on outré Alexander McQueen outfits, despite the marble floors and wood-panel "library," open fires, oils, and fine antiques. The hotel health club is one of the best around, thanks to its good-size pool. Bedrooms are spacious, and most of the marble bathrooms have natural light. ⊠ *Park La., W1A 3AA,* ☎ *020/7499–6363,* ℻ *020/7493–3341. 360 rooms with bath, 70 suites with bath. 3 restaurants, bar, lobby lounge, indoor pool, health club. AE, DC, MC, V. Tube: Marble Arch.*

£££   🏨 **Dukes.** This small, exclusive, Edwardian-style hotel is
  ★   possibly London's quietest hotel, secreted in its own discreet cul-de-sac. It's filled with squashy sofas, oils of assorted dukes, and muted, rich colors, and offers guest rooms recently decorated in patrician, antiques-spattered style, plus the best in personal service (they greet you by name every time). ⊠ *35 St. James's Pl., SW1A 1NY,* ☎ *020/7491–4840,* ℻ *020/7493–1264. 80 rooms with bath. Restaurant, dining room. AE, DC, MC, V. Tube: Green Park.*

£££ 🏨 **Stakis St. Ermins.** Smack-dab in the middle of mostly modern Westminster, this hotel is just a short stroll away from Westminster Abbey. An Edwardian anomaly in the shadow of modern skyscrapers, the hotel is housed in an utterly delightful Edwardian pile, set off around a tiny cul-de-sac courtyard fronted with beasts-rampant gates. The lobby is an extravaganza of Victorian baroque. The less costly of the two restaurants, the Cloisters, has a Jacobean-style salon. Guest rooms are tastefully decorated; some have snug dimensions (but are all the cozier for it). ✉ *Caxton St., SW1H 0QW,* ☎ *020/7222–7888,* ℻ *020/7222–6914. 290 rooms with bath, 7 suites with bath. 2 restaurants, bar, minibars, room service, laundry service. AE, DC, MC, V. Tube: St. James's Park.*

£ 🏨 **Edward Lear.** Once the house of Edward Lear (of "The Owl and the Pussycat" fame), this homey hotel has seen better days, according to several of our readers. Still, triple and family rooms are huge; number 14 is a closet—with peace and quiet at the back. In the brick-wall breakfast room you're served sausages and bacon from the Queen's butcher. ✉ *28–30 Seymour St., W1H 5WD,* ☎ *020/7402–5401,* ℻ *020/7706–3766. 31 rooms, 15 with shower, 4 with full bath. Breakfast room. MC, V. Tube: Marble Arch.*

£ 🏨 **Glynne Court Hotel.** Despite its location, this is a quiet, small hotel, and so handy for late-night runs to Virgin Records, being just off hectic Marble Arch. It's no luxury joint, but it is a clean and pleasant place, with spacious rooms containing hair dryers, phones, TVs, sinks, and tea/coffeemakers, and the management is friendly. In all, it's a good buy—doubles run about £65— for the area. ✉ *41 Great Cumberland Pl., W1H 7LG,* ☎ *020/7262–4344,* ℻ *020/ 7724–2071. 14 rooms with bath. AE, DC, MC, V. Tube: Marble Arch.*

Marylebone

£££ 🏨 **Dorset Square Hotel.** This pair of Regency town houses in Sherlock Holmes territory belongs to the welcome new breed of small, luxurious, privately run hotels. The creation of architect–interior designer husband-and-wife team, Tim and Kit Kemp, this is *House Beautiful* come to life, from marble and mahogany bathrooms to antique lace counterpanes, and the staff bends over backward to accommodate your wishes. For on-the-town jaunts, there's even a vintage Bentley available. ✉ *39–40 Dorset Sq., NW1 6QN,* ☎ *020/7723–7874,* FAX *020/7724–3328. 37 rooms with bath. Restaurant, bar. AE, MC, V. Tube: Baker St.*

££ 🏨 **Durrants.** A hotel since the late 18th century, Durrants occupies a quiet corner almost next to the Wallace Collection. It's of good value for the area, and if you like ye woodpanel, leather-armchair, dark-red-pattern-carpet style of olde Englishness, this will suit you. Bedrooms are wan and motel-like but adequate—the few with no bathrooms are £10 a night cheaper. ✉ *George St., W1H 6BH,* ☎ *020/7935–8131,* FAX *020/7487–3510. 96 rooms, 85 with bath. Restaurant, bar, dining room, lobby lounge. AE, MC, V. Tube: Bond St.*

Bloomsbury, Holborn, Soho, and the City

££££ 🏨 **Covent Garden Hotel.** Relentlessly chic, extra-stylish, this
  ★ is Tim and Kit Kemp's latest extravaganza—a former 1880s-vintage hospital in the midst of the artsy Covent Garden district, now the London home-away-from-home for a melange of off-duty celebrities, actors, and style-mavens. Theatrically baronial, fashionably Victorian, the public rooms will keep even the most picky atmosphere-hunter happy. Guest rooms are *World of Interiors* chic, each showcasing matching-but-mixed couturier fabrics to stunning effect. Antique-style desks are vast, beds are gargantuan, and modern bathrooms feature everything from Philippe Starck bidets to they-*have*-thought-of-everything heated mirrors (steam doesn't stick). The Brasserie is excellent. For taste, in every sense of the word, the Covent Garden is the top. ✉ *10 Monmouth St., WC2H 9HB,* ☎ *020/7806–1000,* FAX *020/7806–1100. 46 rooms with bath, 4 suites with bath. Restaurant, minibars, room service, exercise room, laundry service. AE, MC, V. Tube: Covent Garden.*

££££ 🏨 **The Savoy.** This historic, grand, late-Victorian hotel is
  ★ beloved by wielders of international influence, now as ever. Its celebrated Grill has the premier power-lunch tables; it hosted Elizabeth Taylor's first honeymoon in one of its famous river-view rooms; and it poured the world's first martini in its equally famous American Bar—haunted by

Hemingway, Fitzgerald, Gershwin, et al. The spacious, elegant, bright, and comfortable rooms are furnished with antiques and serviced by valets. A room facing the Thames costs extra, but only the new County Hall Marriott tops that view. Bathrooms have original fittings, with sunflower-size showerheads. Though the Savoy is as grand as they come, the air is tinged with a certain theatrical naughtiness (due in part to the on-premises theater), which goes down well with Hollywood types. ⊠ *The Strand, WC2R 0EU,* ☎ *020/7836–4343,* 𝔽𝔸𝕏 *020/7240–6040. 202 rooms with bath. 3 restaurants, 2 bars, indoor pool, beauty salon, health club. AE, DC, MC, V. Tube: Aldwych.*

£££– 🏨 **Myhotel.** A hotel where tipping is discouraged and where
££££ guests brief the management on their likes and dislikes? Where you have a member of staff assigned to you personally, to see to all your needs? Where a public room is dedicated to inner karma? Yes, here it is, the work of owner Andrew Thrasyvoulou and the frighteningly omniscient Terence Conran with the help of a feng shui designer to check the building for negative energy. Myhotel, Conran's first hotel venture, is evidently aimed at the young, hip traveler who expects his or her hotel to be an experience in itself. It is within easy walking distance of the British Museum, Soho, Covent Garden, and the West End. ⊠ *11–13 Bayley St., Bedford Sq., WC1 B3HD,* ☎ *020/7667–6000,* 𝔽𝔸𝕏 *020/ 7667–6001. 76 rooms with bath. Restaurant, bar, exercise room, library, business services.*

£££   🏨 **Hazlitt's.** The solo Soho hotel is in three connected early
★   18th-century houses, one of which was the essayist William Hazlitt's (1778–1830) last home. It's a friendly place, full of personality, but devoid of such hotel features as elevators, room service, and porterage. Robust antiques are everywhere, assorted prints crowd every wall, a Victorian claw-foot tub sits in all bathrooms. Book way ahead—this is the London address of media people, literary types, and antiques dealers everywhere. ⊠ *6 Frith St., W1V 5TZ,* ☎ *020/7434–1771,* 𝔽𝔸𝕏 *020/7439–1524. 23 rooms with bath. AE, DC, MC, V. Tube: Piccadilly.*

£££   🏨 **The Rookery.** From the bijoux-sized but beautiful rooms in this little hotel you see some of the most ancient parts of London. Just a step away is the Jerusalem Tavern, from where it is said the Knights of St. John left to fight the Crusades back in an earlier millennium. From the magnificent Rook's Nest, the hotel's tower that is a complete duplex suite, you can see both St. Paul's and the Old Bailey. If you look closely, some of Dickens's characters still seem to linger around this district, if they haven't been ousted by the fashionable and wealthy young crowd now busy colonizing the area. Each of the hotel's doubles has an antique four-poster and period pictures, with all the modern appliances tastefully hidden away. The burgeoning nature of the neighborhood means there is a huge choice of restaurants but also many noisy building sites. ⊠ *Peter's La., Cowcross St., EC1M 6DS,* ☎ *020/7336–0931,* ☐ *020/7336–0932. 33 rooms with bath. Bar, business services. AE, MC, V.*

£££–£££ 🔁 **The Kingsley.** On the main street, steps from the British Museum, this is one Edwardian-style hotel that really does feel sweetly old-fashioned, avoiding shabbiness or stuffiness—especially since last year's $6-million refurbishment of this former temperance house. English country-house decor has the strong color schemes currently favored in hotel land, with tea/coffeemakers and free in-house movies among the facilities. ⊠ *Bloomsbury Way, WC1A 2SD,* ☎ *020/7242–5881,* ☐ *020/7831–0225. 138 rooms with bath. Restaurant, bar, meeting rooms. AE, DC, MC, V. Tube: Holborn.*

£££ 🔁 **Fielding.** Tucked away in a quiet alley, this cozy hotel is adored for the homey atmosphere, the continuity of a loyal, friendly staff, and for the convenience of having the Royal Opera House, the theater district, and half of London's restaurants within spitting distance. The bedrooms are all different, shabby-homey rather than chic, and none too spacious, though you can have a suite here for the price of a chain-hotel double. There's no elevator; only one room comes with bathtub (most have showers); and only breakfast is served in the restaurant. ⊠ *4 Broad Ct., Bow St., WC2B 5QZ,* ☎ *020/7836–8305,* ☐ *020/7497–0064. 24 rooms with bath. Bar, breakfast room. AE, DC, MC, V. Tube: Covent Garden.*

£ **The Generator.** This four-year-old youth hostel is easily the grooviest in town, with a friendly, funky vibe and vibrant decor—blue neon and brushed steel downstairs, and upstairs dorm rooms painted in bright blue and orange. The Generator Bar has cheap drinks, and the Fuel Stop cafeteria provides inexpensive meals. Rooms are simple but clean—singles run about £38, twins (there are no doubles) about £24 per person, with prices dropping very low for the ones with multiple beds in them. From October to March are bargain-rate months, too. There are no bathrooms en-suite. ⊠ *MacNaghten House, Compton Pl., WC1H 9SD,* ☎ *0171/388–7666,* FAX *0171/388–7644. 213 rooms without bath. Restaurant, bar. MC, V. Tube: Russell Sq.*

£ 🏨 **London Tower Bridge Travel Inn Capital.** The name may not be snappy, but the price certainly is—practically unbeatable, especially for families. Not exactly central, this brand-new hotel is based in the Tower Hill area, which has good tube connections. Bars, apartments blocks, and restaurants are pouring into this part of London, which not so long ago property developers despaired of. Those hoping for glitz should station themselves farther west, but if a bargain and a different look at London are what you want—or the Millennium Dome and the Tower of London are two of your main destinations—save your pennies and stay here. ⊠ *Tower Bridge Rd., SE1,* ☎ *01582/414341. 196 rooms with bath. Restaurant, bar. AE, MC, V.*

£ 🏨 **Morgan.** In this family-run Georgian row-house hotel, rooms are small and functionally furnished, yet friendly and cheerful overall, with phones and TVs. The five newish apartments are particularly pleasing: three times the size of normal rooms (and an extra £15/night, placing them in the ££ category), complete with eat-in kitchens and private phone lines. ⊠ *24 Bloomsbury St., WC1B 3QJ,* ☎ *020/7636–3735. 15 rooms with bath, 5 apartments. Breakfast room. MC, V. Tube: Russell Sq.*

£ 🏨 **St. Margaret's.** This guest house on a tree-lined Georgian street has been run for many years by a friendly Italian family. You'll find spacious rooms and towering ceilings, and a wonderful location close to Russell Square. The back rooms have a garden view. ⊠ *24 Bedford Pl., WC1B 5JL,* ☎ *0171/636–4277. 64 rooms, 10 with bath. No credit cards. Tube: Goodge St.*

Kensington

££££ 🏨 **Blakes.** This has to be the most exotic hotel in town, the work of Lady Weinberg, a.k.a. Anouska Hempel, '70s-style goddess. A sober, dark-green Victorian exterior belies the arty mix of Biedermeier, bamboo, four-poster beds, and Oriental screens inside, with rooms bedecked in anything from black moiré silk to dove gray or top-to-toe blush pink. Guests tend to be music or movie mavens. Look for her newest hotel, the Hempel, too. ⊠ *33 Roland Gardens, SW7 3PF,* ☎ *020/7370–6701,* ℻ *020/7373–0442. 52 rooms with bath. Restaurant. AE, DC, MC, V. Tube: Gloucester Rd.*

£££ ★ 🏨 **The Gore.** Just down the road from the Albert Hall, this small, very friendly hotel, run by the same people who run Hazlitt's (☞ Soho, *above*), features a similarly eclectic selection of prints, etchings, and antiques—the lobby is something out of a fin-de-siècle Visconti film. Here, though, are spectacular follylike rooms—Room 101 is a Tudor fantasy with a minstrel gallery, stained glass, and four-poster bed. The hotel gets a fun, chic, but partying crowd—so please don't be shocked if you find some cigarette butts in the hallways. ⊠ *189 Queen's Gate, SW7 5EX,* ☎ *020/7584–6601,* ℻ *020/7589–8127. 54 rooms with bath. Brasserie. AE, DC, MC, V. Tube: Gloucester Rd.*

££ 🏨 **Forte Posthouse Kensington.** This large, utilitarian hotel feels like a smaller one and offers extras you wouldn't expect for the reasonable rate and convenient location in a quiet lane off Kensington High Street. The main attraction is the health club, with an 18-m pool, two squash courts, a steam room, and a beauty salon. Standard rooms are on the small side, with plain chain-hotel built-in furnishings. ⊠ *Wrights La., W8 5SP,* ☎ *020/7937–8170,* ℻ *020/7937–8289. 543 rooms with bath. 3 restaurants, 2 bars, indoor pool, health club, baby-sitting. AE, DC, MC, V. Tube: High Street Kensington.*

££ 🏨 **Hotel 167.** This friendly little bed-and-breakfast is a two-minute walk from the V&A, in a grand white-stucco Victorian corner house. The lobby is immediately cheering, with its round marble tables, wrought-iron chairs, palms, and modern paintings; it also does duty as lounge and breakfast room. Bedrooms have a hybrid Victoriana/Ikea style with double-glazed windows (which you need on this noisy road). ⊠ *167 Old Brompton Rd., SW5 0AN,* ☎ *020/7373–0672,* ℻ *020/7373–3360. 19 rooms with bath. Breakfast room. AE, DC, MC, V. Tube: Gloucester Rd.*

£   🏨 **Abbey House.** Next door to the Vicarage (*see* below), Abbey House has been voted "Best Value, Best Quality B&B in London" in several surveys, so you'll have to book well in advance for the doubles that go for £60 here. The place occupies a pretty, white-stucco 1860 Victorian town house—once home to a bishop and an MP before World War II—and overlooks a garden square. Rooms are spacious and have color TVs and washbasins, but every room shares a bath with another. An English breakfast is included in the rates, and a cuppa is complimentary. ⊠ *11 Vicarage Gate, W8,* ☎ *020/7727–2594. 16 rooms with shared bath. No credit cards. Tube: High Street Kensington.*

£   🏨 **Eden Plaza.** When a hotel calls its own rooms "compact," you should imagine a double bed, then add a foot all round, and, yes, that is about the measure of a room here. However, like a cruise-ship stateroom, all you need (closet, mirror, satellite TV, tea/coffeemaker, hair dryer) is creatively secreted. Rooms are double-glazed against noisy Cromwell Road, though color schemes are *loud.* Kids share free or get their own room at half price. ⊠ *68–69 Queensgate, SW7 5JT,* ☎ *020/7370–6111,* 🆕 *020/7370–0932. 62 rooms with bath. Bar. AE, MC, V. Tube: Gloucester Rd.*

£   🏨 **Vicarage.** Spend the cash you save here in the surrounding Kensington antiques shops. This has long been a favorite for the budget-minded—family-owned, set on a leaf-shaded street just off Kensington Church Street, the Vicarage is set in a large white Victorian house. The decor is sweetly anachronistic, full of heavy, dark-stained wood furniture, patterned carpets, and brass pendant lights, and there's a little conservatory. Many of the bedrooms now have TVs. All in all, this still remains a charmer—but readers tell us it's beginning to fray around the edges. ⊠ *10 Vicarage Gate, W8 4AG,* ☎ *020/7229–4030. 19 rooms with shared bath. No credit cards. Tube: High Street Kensington.*

Knightsbridge, Chelsea, and Belgravia

££££   🏨 **Berkeley.** A remarkable mixture of the old and new, the Berkeley stars a splendid penthouse swimming pool that opens to the sky when the weather's good. The bedrooms are decorated by various designers, but tend to be serious

Lodging in Kensington, Knightsbridge, Chelsea and

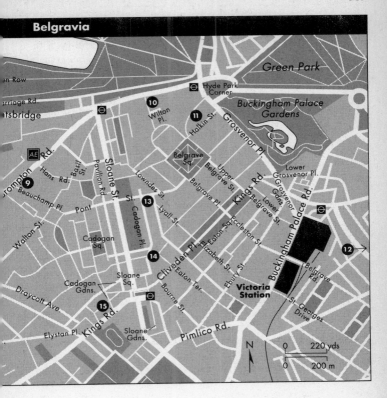

Belgravia

Green Park

Hyde Park Corner

Buckingham Palace Gardens

Wilton Pl.

Halkin St.

Grosvenor Pl.

Belgrave Sq.

Lower Grosvenor Pl.

Sloane St.

Hans Rd.

Basil St.

Pavilion Rd.

Brompton Rd.

Beauchamp Pl.

Pont St.

Lowndes St.

Lyall St.

Belgrave Pl.

Upper Belgrave St.

Kings Rd.

Grosvenor

Lower Belgrave St.

Walton St.

Cadogan Sq.

Cadogan Pl.

Cliveden Pl.

Eaton Pl.

Eaton Ter.

Elizabeth St.

Eccleston St.

Ebury St.

Buckingham Palace Rd.

Belgrave Rd.

Cadogan Gdns.

Sloane Sq.

Bourne St.

Victoria Station

Draycott Ave.

Elystan Pl.

Kings Rd.

Sloane Gdns.

Pimlico Rd.

St. Georges Drive

9 10 11 12 13 14 15

N

0 220 yds
0 200 m

and opulent, have swags of William Morris prints or are plain and masculine with little balconies overlooking the street. All have sitting areas and big, tiled bathrooms with bidets. Its restaurant is Vong, the fabulous Thai/French hybrid cloned from New York. ⊠ *Wilton Pl., SW1X 7RL,* ☎ *020/7235–6000,* ℻ *020/7235–4330. 160 rooms with bath. 2 restaurants, indoor-outdoor pool, beauty salon, health club, cinema. AE, DC, MC, V. Tube: Knightsbridge.*

££££ 🏨 **The Halkin.** This luxurious little place is so contemporary you worry it will be outdated in a couple of years and they'll have to redo the whole thing. Milanese designers were responsible for the clean-cut white marble lobby, and the gray-on-gray bedrooms that light up when you insert your electronic key and contain every high-tech toy you never knew you needed. It might be like living in the Design Museum, except that this place employs some of the friendliest people around—who look pretty good in their white Armani uniforms. ⊠ *Halkin St., SW1X 7DJ,* ☎ *020/7333–1000,* ℻ *020/7333–1100. 41 rooms with bath. Restaurant. AE, DC, MC, V. Tube: Hyde Park Corner.*

£££ 🏨 **Beaufort.** You can practically hear the jingle of Harrods's
★ cash registers from a room at the Beaufort. Actually, "hotel" is a misnomer for this elegant pair of Victorian houses. There's a sitting room instead of reception; guests have a front door key, the run of the drinks cabinet, and even their own phone number. The high-ceiling, generously proportioned rooms are decorated in muted, sophisticated shades to suit the muted, sophisticated atmosphere—but don't worry, you're encouraged by the incredibly sweet staff to feel at home. ⊠ *33 Beaufort Gardens, SW3 1PP,* ☎ *020/7584–5252,* ℻ *020/7589–2834. 28 rooms with bath. AE, DC, MC, V. Tube: Knightsbridge.*

£££ 🏨 **The Pelham.** The second of Tim and Kit Kemp's gorgeous
★ hotels opened in 1989 and is run along exactly the same lines as the Dorset Square (☞ Marylebone, *above*), except that this one looks less town than country. There's 18th-century pine paneling in the drawing room—one of the magnificently handsome hotel salons in the city—flowers galore, quite a bit of glazed chintz, and the odd four-poster and bedroom fireplace. The Pelham stands opposite the South Kensington tube stop, by the big museums, and close to the shops of Knightsbridge, with Kemps supplying an on-site

trendy menu. ⊠ *15 Cromwell Pl., SW7 2LA,* ☎ *020/ 7589–8288,* FAX *020/7584–8444. 37 rooms with bath. Restaurant, pool. AE, MC, V. Tube: South Kensington.*

££–£££ ⊡ **The Diplomat.** From its aristocratically elegant exterior, this hotel looks like a Cecil Beaton stage set: a Wedgwood-white "palazzo" terrace house built by the 19th-century architect Thomas Cubitt, flatiron-shape, and often decked out with hanging flowerpots of geraniums, it is the very picture of Belgravia chic. Inside, the tiny reception area gives way to a vintage elevator and a circular staircase lit by a Regency-era chandelier and topped by a winter-garden dome. Rooms are pleasantly decorated. The heart of Belgravia's 19th-century mansions and mews, the hotel is a small hoof away from the tube stop. ⊠ *2 Chesham St., SW1X 3DT,* ☎ *020/7235–1544,* FAX *020/7259–6153. 27 rooms with bath. Business services. AE, DC, MC, V. Tube: Sloane Sq., Knightsbridge.*

££–£££ ⊡ **The Sloane.** The tiny Sloane is the only hotel we know of in which you can lie in your canopy bed, pick up the phone, and buy the bed—and the phone, too, and the tasty antiques all around you. Nothing so tacky as a price tag besmirches the gorgeous decor; instead, the sweet, young Euro staff harbors a book of price lists at the desk. There's an aerie of a secret roof terrace where meals are served, with upholstered garden furniture and a panorama over Chelsea. ⊠ *29 Draycott Pl., SW3 2SH,* ☎ *020/7581–5757,* FAX *020/ 7584–1348. 12 rooms with bath. Restaurant. AE, DC, MC, V. Tube: Sloane Sq.*

£ ⊡ **London County Hall Travel Inn Capital.** This lacks the river view, but you get an incredible value, with the standard facilities of the cookie-cutter rooms of this chain (the phone number's the central reservation line), viz: TV, tea/coffeemaker, en suite bath/shower and—best of all for families on a budget—foldout beds that let you accommodate two kids at no extra charge. You're looking at £50/night for a family of four, in the shadow of Big Ben. *That's* a bargain. ⊠ *Belvedere Rd., SE1 7PB,* ☎ *01582/414341 or 01582/400024. 312 rooms with bath. Restaurant. AE, MC, V. Tube: Westminster.*

£ ⊡ **Wilbraham.** A lovely grandmother of a hotel, this place is as British as tea and crumpets. It's set not far from swanky Sloane Square, comprises three 19th-century row houses, and is decorated in best shabby-genteel Brit fashion, right down to floral wallpapers and Victorian bric-a-brac. Guest rooms don't have many frills, but there's a pleasant lounge and a restaurant—handy for meeting friends over a glass of sherry. ⊠ *1–5 Wilbraham Pl., SW1,* ☎ *020/7730–8296,* FAX *020/7730–6815. 53 rooms with bath. Restaurant, lounge. No credit cards. Tube: Sloane Sq.*

Bayswater and Notting Hill Gate

£££ 📷 **Abbey Court.** You enter this 1850 building through a stately, double-front portico to find yourself in a luxury bed-and-breakfast filled with Empire furniture, oil portraits, and the odd four-poster bed. Kensington Gardens is close by, or you could save the walk and relax in the pretty conservatory. ⊠ *20 Pembridge Gardens, W2 4DU,* ☎ *020/7221–7518,* FAX *020/7792–0858. 22 rooms with bath. AE, DC, MC, V. Tube: Notting Hill Gate.*

££ 📷 **London Elizabeth.** With one of the prettiest hotel facades in London, this family-owned gem is only steps from Hyde Park and the Lancaster Gate tube (and from rows of depressing, cheap hotels). The facade is one of the most charming in London, and the charm continues inside—foyer and lounge crammed with chintz drapery, lace antimacassars, and little chandeliers. With their palest blue-striped walls, wooden picture rails, and Welsh wool bedspreads or pink cabbage-rose prints and mahogany furniture, the rooms do vary in size, and some lack a full-length mirror, but they all have TV, direct-dial phone, and hair dryer, and they're serviced by an exceptionally charming Anglo-Irish staff. ⊠ *Lancaster Terr., W2 3PF,* ☎ *020/7402–6641,* FAX *020/7224–8900. 55 rooms with bath. Restaurant, bar. AE, DC, MC, V. Tube: Lancaster Gate.*

£ 📷 **Columbia.** The public rooms in these five joined-up Victorians are as big as museum halls. Late at night they contain the hippest band du jour relaxing during their London gig; in the morning, there are sightseers sipping coffee—a unique mix among London's bargain hotels, as this place seems to offer something for everyone. The clean, high-ceiling rooms, some of which are very large (three to four beds)

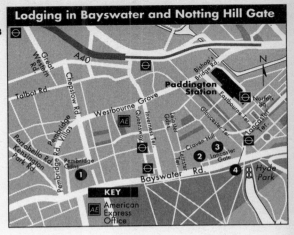

Lodging in Bayswater and Notting Hill Gate

and have park views and balconies, also offer TVs, hair dryers, tea/coffeemakers, direct-dial phones, and safes. Decor tends to teak veneer, khaki-beige-brown color schemes, and avocado bathroom suites, but you can't expect Regency Revival at these prices. ⊠ *95–99 Lancaster Gate, W2 3NS,* ☎ *020/7402–0021,* FAX *020/7706–4691. 103 rooms with bath. Restaurant, bar, meeting rooms. AE, MC, V. Tube: Lancaster Gate.*

£　🏨 **Commodore.** This peaceful hotel of three converted Vic-
★　torians has some amazing rooms for the price—as superior to the regular ones (which usually go to package tour groups) as Harrods is to Kmart. Twenty are miniduplexes, with sleeping gallery (which cost more than the ££ category); all have tea/coffeemakers, hair dryers, and TVs with pay movies. No. 11 is a real duplex, entered through a secret mirrored door. ⊠ *50 Lancaster Gate, W2 3NA,* ☎ *020/ 7402–5291,* FAX *020/7262–1088. 90 rooms with bath. Bar, business services. AE, MC, V. Tube: Lancaster Gate.*

5 Nightlife and the Arts

NIGHTLIFE

Nighttime London has rejuvenated itself in the past few years, with a tangible new spirit of fun abroad on the streets and new hangouts opening at an unprecedented rate. Whatever your pleasure, there's somewhere to go. London's clubs are famously hip, hot, and happening. Music is everywhere. Cabaret and comedy remain favorite ways to wind down. There are also numerous gambling clubs around town— ask your concierge for tips on the best (in most, you have to apply for "membership" 24 hours before playing). All you need remember when you hit the town at night is that regular bars (those without special extended licenses) stop serving alcohol at 11 PM (10:30 on Sun.), and the tubes stop around midnight.

Bars

American Bar. Festooned with a chin-dropping array of collegiate ties, bric-a-brac, and antique toys, this is one of London's most sensational, funhouse interiors. Even if you're not feeling homesick for the other side of the pond, be sure to check out this dazzler. ⊠ *Stafford Hotel, St. James's Pl., SW1A,* ☎ *020/7493–0111.* ⊘ *Weekdays 11 am–midnight, weekends noon–3, 5:30–11:30. AE, MC, V.*

The Atlantic. This vast, glamorous, wood-floor basement was the first central London bar to be granted a late-late alcohol license. The restaurant is more dominant these days, and reserving a table is the only way to get in late on weekends. ⊠ *20 Glasshouse St., W1,* ☎ *020/7734–4888.* ⊘ *Mon.–Sat. noon–3 am, Sun. noon–11:30. AE, MC, V.*

Beach Blanket Babylon. In Notting Hill, close to Portobello Market, this always-packed singles bar is distinguishable by its fanciful decor—like a fairy-tale grotto, or a medieval dungeon, visited by the gargoyles of Notre Dame. ⊠ *45 Ledbury Rd., W11,* ☎ *020/7229–2907.* ⊘ *Daily noon–11. AE, MC, V.*

Cadogan Hotel Bar. One step beyond the door here and you're back in the Edwardian era. You half expect Lillie Langtry, the famed actress and mistress of King Edward VII, to waltz in the door—but then she used to live upstairs. If you feel like toasting Oscar Wilde with his favorite drink, a Hock and Seltzer, you'd better do it elsewhere—poor Oscar was arrested in this very bar that fateful day. ⊠ *Cadogan Hotel, Sloane St., SW1,* ☎ *020/7235–7141.* ⊗ *Daily 11–11. AE, MC, V.*

The Library. The comfortable, self-consciously "period" bar at the swanky Lanesborough Hotel harbors a collection of ancient cognacs, made in years when something important happened. Don't ask for a brandy Alexander. ⊠ *Hyde Park Corner, SW1,* ☎ *020/7259–5599.* ⊗ *Mon.–Sat. 11–11, Sun. noon–2:30 and 7–10:30. AE, DC, MC, V.*

Cabaret

Comedy Store. The improv factory where the United Kingdom's funniest stand-ups cut their teeth has now relocated to a bigger and better space. ⊠ *Haymarket House, Oxendon St., SW1,* ☎ *020/7344–4444, 01426/914433 for information.* ⊠ *£11–£13.* ⊗ *Shows Tues.–Thurs., Sun. at 8, Fri.–Sat. at 8 and midnight. AE, MC, V.*

Madame Jo Jo's. By no means devoid of straight spectators, this place has long been one of the most fun drag cabarets in town—civilized of atmosphere, despite barechested bar boys. Many nights are club nights, so call ahead. ⊠ *8 Brewer St.,* ☎ *020/7287–1414.* ⊠ *£6 Mon.–Thurs., £8 Fri.–Sat.* ⊗ *Doors open at 10 pm; shows at 12:15 and 1:15.*

Clubs

Camden Palace. It would be difficult to find a facial wrinkle in this huge place, even if you could see through the laser lights and find your way around the three floors of bars at this rejuvenated and hip-once-more megaclub. ⊠ *1A Camden High St., NW1,* ☎ *020/7387–0428.* ⊠ *£9–£15.* ⊗ *Tues.–Thurs. 10 pm–midnight, Fri.–Sat. 10 pm–6 am. AE, MC, V.*

Heaven. London's premier (mainly) gay club is the best place for dancing wildly for hours. A state-of-the-art laser show and a large, throbbing dance floor complement a labyrinth of quieter bars and lounges. ⊠ *Under the Arches, Villiers St., WC2,* ☎ *020/7839–2520.* ▭ *£1–£10.* ⊙ *Weekdays 10:30 pm–3:30 am, Sat. 11:30 pm–6 am. AE, DC, MC, V.*

Stringfellows. Peter Stringfellow's first London nightclub is not at all hip, but is very glitzy, with mirrored walls, a light show, and an expensive art deco–style restaurant. Suburbanites and middle-age swingers frequent it. ⊠ *16–19 Upper St. Martin's La., WC2,* ☎ *020/7240–5534.* ▭ *£10 before 10 pm, £15 after.* ⊙ *Mon.–Thurs. 7 pm–3:30 am, Fri.–Sat. 8 pm–3:30 am. AE, DC, MC, V.*

Jazz

Jazz Café. This palace of high-tech cool in a converted bank in bohemian Camden is the essential hangout for mainstream jazz, world beat, and younger crossover performers. It's steps from Camden Town tube station. ⊠ *5–7 Pkwy., NW1,* ☎ *020/7916–6060.* ▭ *£8–£10, depending on band.* ⊙ *Mon.–Thurs. 7 pm–1 am, Fri.–Sat. 7 pm–2 am, Sun. 7 pm–midnight. AE, DC, MC, V.*

Pizza Express. It may seem strange, but this is one of London's principal jazz venues, with music every night except Monday in the basement restaurant. The subterranean interior is darkly lit, the lineups (often featuring visiting U.S. performers) are interesting, and the Italian-style thin-crust pizzas are great! Eight other branches also have live music; check the listings for details. ⊠ *10 Dean St., W1,* ☎ *020/7437–9595.* ▭ *£8–£20, depending on band.* ⊙ *From noon for food; music Mon.–Sun. 9 pm–midnight. AE, DC, MC, V. Tube: Tottenham Court Rd.*

Ronnie Scott's. This legendary Soho jazz club, since its opening in the early '60s, has attracted all the big names. It's usually packed and hot, but the atmosphere can't be beat, and it's probably still London's best, even since the sad departure of its eponymous founder and saxophonist. ⊠ *47 Frith St., W1,* ☎ *020/7439–0747.* ▭ *£15–£20 nonmembers.* ⊙ *Mon.–Sat. 8:30 pm–3 am, Sun. 7:30–11:30 pm. Reservations essential. AE, DC, MC, V.*

Rock

The Astoria. Very central, quite hip, this place hosts bands with a buzz, plus late club nights. ✉ *157 Charing Cross Rd., W1,* ☎ *020/7434–0403.* ✇ *£10–£12.* ☉ *Check listings for opening times. No credit cards.*

The Forum. This ex-ballroom with balcony and dance floor packs in the customers and consistently attracts the best medium-to-big-name performers, too. Get the tube to Kentish Town, then follow the hordes. ✉ *9–17 Highgate Rd., NW5,* ☎ *020/7344–0044.* ✇ *£8–£12.* ☉ *Most nights 7–11. AE, MC, V.*

THE ARTS

London's nightlife scene is populated by here-today-gone-tomorrow boîtes and clubs, with trendsetters constantly on the move. In contrast, London's arts scenes have entertainment options that, by and large, remain forever sparkling. At the top of anyone's must-do list, of course, are the Broadway shows presented at the West End theaters, the gala nights offered by the Royal Opera and Ballet, and the best performances of the Bard given by the Royal Shakespeare Company and at the new Shakespeare's Globe Theatre.

Ballet

The Royal Opera House is the traditional home of the world-famous **Royal Ballet,** and the tutus and ribboned shoes will soon be tripping onto its stage once more. The beloved opera house has been closed for two years so its infrastructure could be modernized, but the reopening of the Opera House on December 1, 1999, will once more give the company a permanent home. Until then, the troupe will be appearing at the Sadler's Wells Theater and at the Royal Festival Hall. A new pricing structure should bring tickets for both opera and ballet into the affordable bracket for a good percentage of the performances. Check with the **Royal Opera House** for further information. **The London City Ballet** is normally based at **Sadler's Wells Theatre,** though this is yet another theater due for renovation for the millennium. Check the *Time Out* and newspaper listings for the latest up-dates. **The Place** is indeed the place for contemporary dance, physical theater, and the avant garde. Prices at these performances are much cheaper than for those at Covent Garden.

Concerts

Ticket prices for symphony concerts range from £5–£45. International guest appearances usually mean higher prices; reserve well in advance for such performances. Those with-out reservations might go to the hall half an hour before the performance for a chance at returns.

The London Symphony Orchestra is in residence at the **Bar-bican Arts Centre;** the Philharmonia and the Royal Phil-harmonic also perform here. The **South Bank Centre,** which includes the Royal Festival Hall, Queen Elizabeth Hall, and the small Purcell Room, forms another major venue. Be-tween the Barbican and South Bank, there are concert per-formances every night of the year. The Barbican also features chamber music concerts with such smaller orchestras as the City of London Sinfonia.

To experience a great British institution, try for the **Royal Albert Hall** during "The Proms," (July–September). Un-fortunately, demand for tickets is so high that you must enter a lottery. For regular "proms," tickets run £3–£30; special "promenade" (standing) tickets usually cost half the price of normal tickets and are available at the hall on the night of the concert. Note, too, that the concerts have begun to be jumbo-screen broadcast in Hyde Park, but even here a seat on the grass requires a paid ticket. In summer, don't miss the outdoor concerts (complete with fireworks) by the lake at elegant Kenwood House (Hampstead Heath; ☎ 020/ 7973–3427)—usually held every Saturday from mid-June to early September—or the opera in Holland Park.

Numerous lunchtime concerts take place across London in smaller concert halls and churches. They feature string quartets, vocalists, jazz ensembles, and gospel choirs. **St. Martin-in-the-Fields** is a particularly popular location.

Performances usually begin about 1 PM and last an hour. Some are free.

Movies

Despite the video invasion, West End movies still thrive. The largest major first-run houses are found in the Leicester Square/Piccadilly Circus area, where tickets average £8. Monday and matinees are usually half price; lines are also shorter. The best revival house is the **National Film Theatre,** part of the South Bank Centre (☞ The South Bank *in* Chapter 2), which screens big past hits, plus work neglected by the more ticket-sales-dependent houses, since it comes under the auspices of the British Film Institute. The main events of the annual London Film Festival take place here in the fall. Daily membership costs 40p.

Opera

The main venue for Opera in London is the fabled **Royal Opera House,** which ranks with the Metropolitan Opera House in New York—in every way, except, surprisingly, expense. Long castigated in Britain for its outrageous ticket prices, the Opera House has adopted a new policy and pledged to lower its prices for the new season, premiering December 1999 with the gala reopening of the renovated Royal Opera House in Covent Garden. Closed since 1997, the famous theater promises to reopen with a fanfare with both resident companies and Placido Domingo performing an opening Gala, to celebrate the return of The House, as it is known. Tickets will cost between £8–£100. Conditions of purchase vary—call for information. For the 1998–99 season, most productions for the company should be concentrated in the newly refurbished Sadler's Wells Theatre. Call the box office number for information and current schedules.

English-language productions are staged at the **Coliseum,** home of the English National Opera Company. Prices here range from £8 for standing room to about £55 for the best seats, and productions are often innovative and exciting.

Theater

One of the nonpareil experiences the city has to offer is great theater. London's theater scene consists, broadly, of the state-subsidized companies, the Royal National Theatre and the Royal Shakespeare Company; the commercial West End, equivalent to Broadway; and the Fringe—small, experimental companies. Another category could be added: known in the weekly listings magazine *Time Out* as Off-West End, these are shows staged at the longer-established fringe theaters.

Most theaters have a matinee twice a week (Wed. or Thurs., and Sat.) and nightly performances at 7:30 or 8, except Sunday. Prices vary: expect to pay from £6 for an upper balcony seat to at least £25 for the stalls (orchestra) or dress circle. Reserve tickets at the box office, over the phone by credit card (numbers in the phone book or newspaper marked "cc" are for credit-card reservations), or (for a couple of pounds) through ticket agents such as **First Call** (☎ 020/7420–0000). To reserve before your trip use **Ticketmaster**'s U.S. booking line (☎ 800/775–2525), or reserve once in ⊠ London (☎ 020/7344–0055). Half-price, same-day tickets are sold for cash only (subject to availability) from the **Society of London Theatres (SOLT)** kiosk on the southwest corner of Leicester Square, open Monday–Saturday, 2–6:30, Sunday noon–3, and from noon on matinee days; there is a £2 service charge. There is always a long line. The "half-price" tickets here are often the orchestra seats. If you wish to snag a cheaper, balcony seat, it may be wiser to go directly to the theater box office. Larger hotels have reservation services but add hefty service charges.

The **Royal Shakespeare Company** and the **Royal National Theatre Company** perform at London's two main arts complexes, the **Barbican Centre** and **The Royal National Theatre,** respectively. Both companies mount consistently excellent productions and are usually a safe option for anyone having trouble choosing which play to see. A great hue-and-cry has gone up concerning the RSC's plans to tour the provinces during summer months—thereby depriving many tourists from seeing the best of all theater companies. Plans are still tentative at press time, so be sure to telephone before departing home. Happily, however, it is exactly

Theaters and Concert Halls Around West End

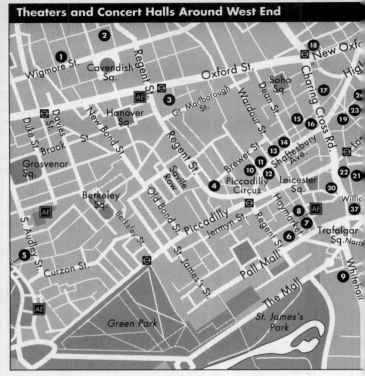

Adelphi, **35**
Albery, **22**
Aldwych, **30**
Apollo, **11**
Barbican Arts
Centre (RSC), **42**
Cambridge, **23**
Coliseum, **21**
Comedy, **8**

Dominion, **18**
Donmar
Warehouse, **24**
Drury Lane
(Theatre
Royal), **28**
Duchess, **32**
Fortune, **27**
Garrick, **20**

Gielgud, **13**
Haymarket, **7**
Her Majesty's, **6**
London
Palladium, **3**
Lyric, **10**
Mermaid, **41**
National Film
Theatre, **44**

New London, **26**
Old Vic, **40**
Open–Air
Theatre, **2**
Palace, **16**
Phoenix, **17**
Piccadilly, **4**
Players, **36**
Playhouse, **38**

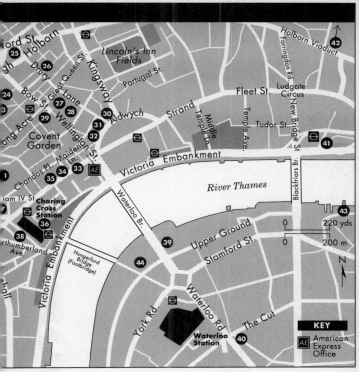

Prince Edward, **15**	Royal Opera House, **29**	Shakespeare's Globe Theatre, **43**
Prince of Wales, **12**	St. Martin-in-the-Fields, **37**	South Bank Arts Centre, **44**
Queens, **14**	St. Martin's, **19**	Strand, **31**
Royal Albert Hall, **5**	Savoy, **33**	Vaudeville, **34**
Royal National Theatre, **39**	Shaftesbury, **25**	Whitehall, **9**
		Wigmore Hall, **1**

during those summer months (and only then), that you can now see the Bard served up in his most spectacular manifestation—at the new open-air reconstruction of **Shakespeare's Globe Theatre** in Southwark, across the Thames from St. Paul's Cathedral. This re-creation of an open-air Elizabethan-era theater offers a summer season only, with a repertory of four plays given each season (☞ Shakespeare's Globe *in* Chapter 2). Most of London's theaters are in the neighborhood nicknamed Theatreland, around the Strand and Shaftesbury Avenue. For further information about current and future theatrical events in London, use the Web site www.officiallondontheatre.co.uk, or contact the **Society of London Theatres** (✉ Bedford Chambers, The Piazza, Covent Garden, London WC2 E8HQ, ☎ 020/7836–0971).

Performance Venue Addresses

Below is the contact information for the main repetory theaters and concert halls listed above.

Barbican (RSC), ✉ *Barbican, EC2Y 8DS,* ☎ *020/7638–8891 or 020/7628–2295. Tube: Moorgate.*

Coliseum, ✉ *St. Martin's La., WC2N 4ES,* ☎ *020/7632–8300. Tube: Leicester Sq.*

The Place, ✉ *17 Duke's Rd, WC1,* ☎ *020/7387–0031. Tube: Euston.*

Royal Albert Hall, ✉ *Kensington Gore, SW7 2AP,* ☎ *020/7589–8212. Tube: South Kensington.*

Royal National Theatre (Cottesloe, Lyttelton, and Olivier), ✉ *South Bank Centre, SE1 9PX,* ☎ *020/7928–2252. Tube: Waterloo.*

Royal Opera House, ✉ *Covent Garden, WC2E 9DD,* ☎ *020/7304–4000. Tube: Covent Garden.*

Sadler's Wells Theatre, ✉ *Rosebery Ave., EC1R 4TN,* ☎ *020/7713–6000. Tube: Angel.*

Shakespeare's Globe Theatre (South Bank), ✉ *New Globe Walk, Bankside,* ☎ *020/7928–6406. Tube: Blackfriars, then walk across Blackfriars Bridge.*

South Bank Centre, ✉ *South Bank, SE1 8XX,* ☎ *020/ 7960–4233. Tube: Waterloo.*

St. Martin-in-the-Fields, ✉ *Trafalgar Sq., WC2N 4JJ,* ☎ *020/ 7839–1930. Tube: Charing Cross.*

6 Outdoor Activities and Sports

Participant Sports

Gyms

Jubilee Hall (✉ 30 The Piazza, Covent Garden, WC2, ☎ 020/7379–0008). The day rate is £6.50, monthly £49.50, at this very crowded but happening and super-well-equipped central gym. **The Peak** (✉ Hyatt Carlton Tower Hotel, 2 Cadogan Pl., SW1, ☎ 020/7235–1234). This hotel club has top equipment, great ninth-floor views over Knightsbridge, a beauty spa, and a sauna—with TV. Day memberships are no longer available, but the 20-visit pass for £800 is fully transferrable, so a whole family could share one—as long as they use up the visits within the 6-month expiration date.

Running

Green Park and **St. James's Park** are convenient to the Piccadilly hotels. It's about 2 mi around both. **Hyde Park** and **Kensington Gardens** together supply a 4-mi perimeter route, or you can do a 2½-mi run in Hyde Park alone if you start at Hyde Park Corner or Marble Arch and encircle the Serpentine. Near the Park Lane hotels, **Regent's Park** has the Outer Circle loop, measuring about 2½ mi. **London Hash House Harriers** (☎ 020/8995–7879) or the **City Hash House Hotline** (☎ 020/8749–2646) organize noncompetitive hour-long runs (£1) around interesting parts of town, with loops and checkpoints built in.

Swimming

Ironmonger Row (✉ Ironmonger Row, EC1, ☎ 020/7253–4011). This 33-by-12-yard City pool is in a '30s complex that includes a Turkish bath. **Oasis** (✉ 32 Endell St., WC2, ☎ 020/7831–1804) is just that, with a heated pool, open May–September, right in Covent Garden, and a 30-by-10-yard one indoors.

Spectator Sports

For information on London's sports clubs and facilities, call **Sportsline,** weekdays 10–6, ☎ 020/7222–8000.

Cricket

Lord's (✉ St. John's Wood, NW8, ☎ 020/7289–1611) has been hallowed turf for worshipers of England's summer game since 1811. The World Series of cricket, the Tests, is played here, but tickets are hard to procure. One-day international and top-class county matches can usually be seen by lining up on the day of the match.

Running

The **Flora London Marathon** starts at 9 AM on the third Sunday in April, with some 25,000 athletes running from Blackheath or Greenwich to Westminster Bridge or the Mall. Entry forms for the following year are available starting in May (☎ 01891/234234).

Soccer

Three British football (soccer) clubs competing in the **Premier League** are particularly popular: **Arsenal** (✉ Avenell Rd., Highbury, N5, ☎ 020/7359–0131), **Chelsea** (✉ Stamford Bridge, Fulham Rd., SW6, ☎ 020/7385–5545), and **Tottenham Hotspur** (✉ White Hart La., 748 High Rd., N17, ☎ 020/8808–3030). More than likely you won't see a hint of the infamous hooliganism but will be quite carried away by the electric atmosphere only a vast football crowd can generate.

Tennis

The **Wimbledon Lawn Tennis Championships** is, of course, one of the top four Grand Slam events of the tennis year. There's a lottery system for advance purchase of tickets. To apply, send a self-addressed, stamped envelope between October and December (✉ All England Lawn Tennis & Croquet Club, Box 98, Church Rd., Wimbledon SW19 5AE, ☎ 020/8946–2244), then fill in the application form, and hope. Alternatively, during the last-week-of-June, first-week-of-July tournament, tickets collected from departed spectators are resold (profits go to charity). These can provide grandstand seats with plenty to see—play continues till dusk. Call the LTB **Wimbledon Information Line** (☎ 01839/123417); it costs 49p per minute from the beginning of June.

7 Shopping

NAPOLÉON MUST HAVE KNOWN what he was talking about when he called Britain a nation of shopkeepers. No question about it, the finest emporiums are in London, still. You can shop like royalty at Her Majesty's glove maker, discover an uncommon Toby jug in a Kensington antiques shop, or find a leather-bound edition of *Wuthering Heights* on Charing Cross Road. If you have a yen to keep up with the Windsors, head for stores proclaiming they are "By Appointment" to H.M. The Queen—or to the Queen Mother, Prince Philip, or the Prince of Wales. The fashion-forward crowd favors places like Harvey Nichols, shrine-of-all-shrines for *Absolutely Fabulous*'s Patsy and Edina. If you have only limited time, zoom in on one or two of the West End's grand department stores, such as Harrods or Marks & Spencer, where you'll find enough booty for your entire gift list. Below is a brief introduction to the major shopping centers.

CHELSEA
Chelsea centers on the King's Road, once synonymous with ultrafashion; it still harbors some designer boutiques, plus antiques and home furnishings stores.

COVENT GARDEN
This something-for-everyone neighborhood has chain clothing stores and top designers, stalls selling crafts, and shops selling gifts of every type—bikes, kites, tea, herbs, beads, hats, you name it.

KENSINGTON
Kensington's main drag, Kensington High Street, is a smaller, classier version of Oxford Street, with some larger stores at the eastern end. Try Kensington Church Street for expensive antiques, plus a little fashion.

KNIGHTSBRIDGE
Neighboring Knightsbridge has Harrods, of course, but also Harvey Nichols, the top clothes stop, and many expensive designers' boutiques along Sloane Street, Walton Street, and Beauchamp Place.

In Mayfair are the two Bond streets, Old and New, with desirable dress designers, jewelers, and fine art. South Molton Street has high-price, high-style fashion—especially at Brown's—and the tailors of Savile Row are of worldwide repute.

At right angles to Oxford Street is Regent Street, with possibly London's most pleasant department store, Liberty, plus Hamleys, the capital's toy mecca. Shops around once-famous Carnaby Street stock designer youth paraphernalia and 57 varieties of T-shirt.

Here the English gentleman buys everything but the suit (which is from Savile Row): handmade hats, shirts, and shoes, silver shaving kits and hip flasks; you'll also find the world's best cheese shop, Paxton & Whitfield. Nothing in this neighborhood is cheap, in any sense.

Specialty Stores

London is full of wonderful and also offbeat merchandise. We have space to include only a few stores in each category.

Antiques
Antiquarius (⊠ 131–141 King's Rd., SW3, ☎ 020/7351–5353), at the Sloane Square end of the King's Road, is an indoor antiques market with more than 200 stalls offering a wide variety of collectibles, including things that won't bust your baggage allowance: Art Deco brooches, meerschaum pipes, silver salt cellars. **Grays Antique Market** (⊠ 58 Davies St., W1, ☎ 020/7629–7034) is conveniently central. It assembles dealers specializing in everything from Sheffield plates to Chippendale furniture. Bargains are not impossible, and proper pedigrees are guaranteed.

Books and Records
Charing Cross Road is London's "booksville," with a couple of dozen antiquarian booksellers, and many new bookshops, too.

140

Shopping A (Mayfair, Soho, and Covent Garden)

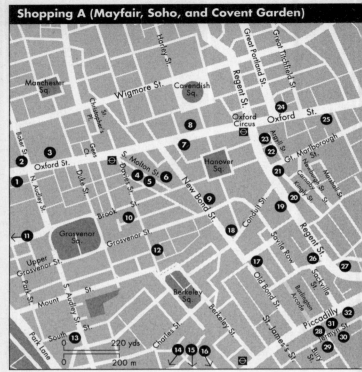

Aquascutum, **27**	The Cross, **11**	Gabriel's Wharf, **44**	Herbert Johnson, **17**
Asprey and Garrard, **18**	Dance Books, **36**	Gray's Antique Market/Gray's Mews, **10**	HMV, **7**
Bell, Book and Radmall, **35**	Favourbrook, **31**		Jigsaw, **9**
	Floris, **30**	Grosvenor Prints, **49**	Jimmy Choo, **14**
Browns, **4**	Forbidden Planet, **54**	Hamleys, **20**	John Lewis, **8**
Burberrys, **19, 34**	Fortnum & Mason, **28**	Hatchards, **32**	Koh Samui, **41**
Butler and Wilson, **5**	Foyles, **52**	Hat Shop, **45**	Laura Ashley, **22**
Cecil Court, **40**			Les Senteurs, **15**

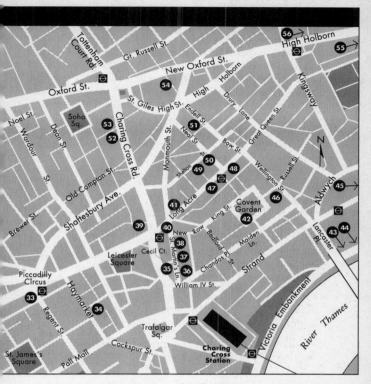

Leslie Craze Gallery, **56**	Outlaws Club, **51**	Selfridges, **3**	Turnbull & Asser, **29**
Liberty, **21**	OXO Tower, **43**	Selina Blow/Lulu Guiness/Camilla Ridley, **16**	Vivienne Westwood, **12**
London Silver Vaults, **55**	Ozwald Boateng, **26**	Stanfords, **48**	Virgin Megastore, **1**
Lush, **42**	Paul Smith, **47**	Tea House, **50**	Warehouse, **23**
Marchpane, **37**	Pellicano, **6**	Thomas Goode, **13**	Waterstone's, **53**
Marks & Spencer, **2, 25**	Penhaligon's, **46**	Tower Records, **33**	Zwemmer, **39**
Miss Selfridge, **24**	Pleasures of Times Past, **38**		

Cecil Court. Just off the Charing Cross Road is this pedes-
trians-only lane where every shop is a specialty bookstore.
Bell, Book and Radmall (⌧ No. 4, ☎ 020/7240–2161) has
quality antiquarian volumes and specializes in modern first
editions; **Marchpane** (⌧ No. 16, ☎ 020/7836–8661) stocks
covetable rare and antique illustrated children's books;
Dance Books (⌧ No. 9, ☎ 020/7836–2314) has—yes—
dance books; and **Pleasures of Times Past** (⌧ No. 11, ☎
020/7836–1142) indulges the collective nostalgia for Victoriana. **Forbidden Planet** (⌧ 71 New Oxford St., WC1,
☎ 020/7836–4179) is the place for sci-fi, fantasy, horror,
and comic books. **Foyles** (⌧ 119 Charing Cross Rd., ☎
020/7437–5660) is especially large—so vast it can be con-
fusing, but it is the place to come to find almost anything.
Hatchards (⌧ 187–188 Piccadilly, WC2, ☎ 020/7439–
9921) has not only a huge stock, but also a well-informed
staff to help you choose. **Stanfords** (⌧ 12 Long Acre, WC2,
☎ 020/7836–1321) is the place for travel books and, especially, maps. **Waterstone's** (⌧ 121–125 Charing Cross
Rd., ☎ 020/7434–4291) is part of an admirable, and expanding, chain with long hours and a program of author
readings and signings. **Zwemmer** (⌧ 24 Litchfield St.,
WC2, ☎ 020/7240–4158), just off Charing Cross Road,
is for art books, with various specialist offshoots.

London created the great megastores that have taken over
the globe. These three stock most, if not all, of your CD,
record, and video needs. **HMV** (⌧ 150 Oxford St., W1, ☎
020/7631–3423) has branches everywhere, but make a
special trip to the HMV (did you know this stands for His
Majesty's Voice?) flagship store for the widest selection.
There are lots of autograph sessions and free shows, too.

Tower Records (⌧ 1 Piccadilly Circus, W1, ☎ 020/7439–
2500) doesn't carry records—go figure. Overlook that and
you'll find its specialty departments are some of the best
in London.

Virgin Megastore (⌧ 14–16 Oxford St., W1, ☎ 020/7631–
1234) is Richard Branson's pride and joy (though his New
York City store is even bigger). It's nice to have it all under
one roof, we suppose—all 8 billion selections.

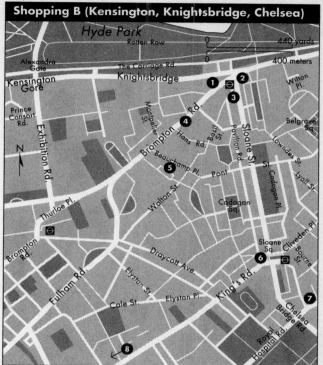

Shopping B (Kensington, Knightsbridge, Chelsea)

Antiquarius, **8**

Browns, **3**

David Linley
Furniture, **7**

General
Trading Co., **6**

Harrods, **4**

Harvey
Nichols, **2**

Map House, **5**

Scotch
House, **1**

China and Glass

Thomas Goode (⊠ 19 S. Audley St., W1, ☎ 020/7499–2823)
has vast ranges of formal china and lead crystal—including English Wedgwood and Minton—and is not only London's finest, but one of the world's top shops.

Clothing

See also Menswear *and* Womenswear, *below.*

Aquascutum (⊠ 100 Regent St., W1, ☎ 020/7734–6090)
is known for its classic raincoats but also stocks the garments to wear underneath, for both men and women. Style keeps up with the times but is firmly on the safe side, making this a good bet for solvent professionals with an anti–fashion victim attitude. **Burberry's** (⊠ 161–165 Regent St., W1, ☎ 020/7734–4060; ⊠ 18–22 The Haymarket, SW1, ☎ 020/7930–3343) tries to evoke an English Heritage ambience, with mahogany closets and stacks of neatly folded neckerchiefs alongside the trademark "Burberry Check" tartan, which adorns—in addition to those famous raincoat linings—scarves, umbrellas, and even shortbread tins in the provisions line. **Marks & Spencer** (⊠ 458 Oxford St., W1, ☎ 020/7935–7954, and branches) is a major chain of stores that's an integral part of the British way of life—sturdy practical clothes, good materials, and workmanship. Dukes to dustmen buy their underwear here. The **Scotch House** (⊠ 2 Brompton Rd., SW3, ☎ 020/7581–2151), as you'd guess, is the place to buy your kilts, tartan scarves, and argyle socks without going to Edinburgh. It's also well stocked with cashmere and accessories.

Crafts

David Linley Furniture (⊠ 60 Pimlico Rd., SW1, ☎ 020/7730–7300) is the outpost for Viscount Linley—the only gentleman in the kingdom who can call the Queen "Auntie" and, more importantly, one of the finest furniture designers of today. The large pieces are suitably expensive, but small desk accessories and objets d'art are also available. The **OXO Tower** (⊠ Bargehouse St., ☎ 020/7401–3610) is now fully functioning as the city's most exciting new place to shop for handmade goods. Studios and shops are open Tuesday–Sunday 11–6. Nearby older sister **Gabriel's Wharf** (⊠ Upper Ground, SE1, ☎ 020/7620–0544) is still a collection of craftspeople in a cute, brightly painted village near the South Bank Centre, who sell porcelain, jewelry, mirrors, clothes, toys, papier-mâché wares and more. **Lesley Craze Gallery** (⊠ 33-35 Clerkenwell Green, EC1, ☎ 020/7608–0393) has cornered a market in a fashionable area. You'll find the most exquisite jewelry to drool over, by some 100 young British designers, who are already teaming up with the fashion stars of the clothes catwalks. The adjacent Craze 2 and C2+ specialize in nonprecious metals and sumptuous scarves and textiles.

Gifts

The Cross (⊠ 141 Portland Rd., W11, ☎ 0171/727–6760) is a thoughtful, ultrachic shop with something to suit everyone—even your pet pooch. This place is big with the high-style crowd, thanks to its ambience (bleached-beach house), its hedonistic, beautiful things (silk scarves, brocade bags, embroidered chinoiserie, jeweled butterflies by Jade Jagger), and its location—bang in the middle of Portobello–cum–Holland Park, London's latest "new" area. **Floris** (⊠ 89 Jermyn St., W1, ☎ 020/7930–2885) is probably the most beautiful shop in London, with 19th-century glass and Spanish mahogany showcases filled with swan's-down powder puffs, cut-glass bottles, and faux tortoiseshell combs. Queen Victoria used to daub her favorite Floris fragrance on her lace handkerchief. **Fortnum & Mason** (⊠ 181 Piccadilly, W1, ☎ 020/7734–8040), the Queen's grocer, is, paradoxically, the most egalitarian of gift stores, with plenty of irresistibly packaged luxury foods, stamped with the gold "By Appointment" crest, for less than £5. Try the teas, preserves, blocks of chocolate, tins of pâté, or turtle soup. The store's uniformed wait staff and its High Tea, served on premises, are marvels. **General Trading Company** (⊠ 144 Sloane St., SW1, ☎ 020/7730–0411) "does" just about every upper-class wedding gift list, but caters also to slimmer pockets with its merchandise shipped from far shores (as the name suggests) but moored securely to English taste. **Hamleys** (⊠ 188–196 Regent St., W1, ☎ 020/7734–3161) has six floors of toys and games for both children and adults. **Les Senteurs** (⊠ 227 Ebury St., SW1, ☎ 0171/730–2322) is an intimate, unglossy gem of a perfumery run by a French family and sells some of the more little-known yet most wonderfully timeless fragrances in town, such as "Creed," worn by Josephine, wife of Emperor Napoleon.

Lush (⊠ 7 The Piazza Court, Covent Garden, WC2, ☎ 020/7240–4570.) The trendiest body-care shop in town sells delicious bath and shower potions, handmade every week. Don't leave London without a supply of Tisty Tosty Ballastics—heart-shape bath bombs. Way cool! Besides this Covent Garden store, there's another location in Chelsea. **Penhaligon's** (⊠ 41 Wellington St., WC2, ☎ 020/7836–2150) was established by William Penhaligon, court barber to Queen Victoria, and parfumier to Lord Rothschild and Winston Churchill. The **Tea House** (⊠ 15A Neal St., WC2, ☎ 020/7240–7539) purveys everything to do with the British national drink; you can dispatch your entire gift list here and delight in what the term "teaphernalia" implies, i.e., strainers, trivets, infusers, and such.

Jewelry

Asprey & Garrard (⊠ 165–169 New Bond St., W1, ☎ 020/7493–6767) has been described as the "classiest and most luxurious shop in the world." It offers a range of exquisite jewelry and gifts, both antique and modern. Owned by the Sultan of Brunei's family, Asprey joined forces with Royal jewellers, Garrard, which moved its operation from Regent Street in summer '98 and is also owned by the Sultan. **Butler and Wilson** (⊠ 20 S. Molton St., W1, ☎ 020/7409–2955) has irresistible costume jewelry displayed against dramatic black, and is especially strong on diamanté, jet, and French gilt. **London Silver Vaults** (⊠ Chancery La., WC2, ☎ 020/7242–5506) has 36 dealers specializing in antique silver and jewelry in a building that used to be a safety deposit during Queen Victoria's reign. The **Outlaws Club** (⊠ 49 Endell St., WC2, ☎ 020/7379–6940) stocks the work of about 100 designers, with prices ranging from a few pounds up to £200. It's pretty avant-garde and has been a favorite with fashion writers for a decade.

Menswear

Favourbrook (⊠ 18 Piccadilly Arcade, W1, ☎ 020/7491–2337) tailors exquisite, handmade vests and jackets, ties and cummerbunds. There's a selection made up for both men and women, or order your own *Four Weddings and a Funeral* outfit. **Herbert Johnson** (✉ 54 St James's St., W1, ☎ 020/7408–1174) is one of a handful of gentleman's hatters who still know how to construct deerstalkers, bowlers, flat caps, and panamas—all the classic headgear, and Ascot-worthy hats for women, too. **Ozwald Boateng** (✉ 9 Vigo St., W1, ☎ 0171/734–6868) is one of the new breed of bespoke tailors whom you will not find on Savile Row but on the fringe. His made-to-measure suits are sought after by rock luminaries for their shock-color linings as well as great classic cuts. **Paul Smith** (✉ 41 Floral St., WC2, ☎ 020/7379–7133) is your man if you don't want to look outlandish but you're bored with plain pants and sober jackets. Sir Paul McCartney is a famous customer. **Turnbull & Asser** (✉ 70 Jermyn St., W1, ☎ 020/7930–0502) is *the* custom shirtmaker. Unfortunately for those of average means, the first order must be for a minimum of six shirts, from about £100 each. But there's a range of less expensive, still exquisitely made ready-to-wear shirts, too.

Prints

Grosvenor Prints (✉ 28 Shelton St., WC2, ☎ 020/7836–1979) sells antiquarian prints, with an emphasis on views and architecture of London—and dogs. The **Map House** (✉ 54 Beauchamp Pl., SW3, ☎ 020/7589–4325) has antique maps from a few pounds to several thousand, but the shop also has excellent reproductions of maps and prints, especially of botanical subjects and cityscapes.

Womenswear

Browns (✉ 23–27 South Molton St., W1, ☎ 020/7491–7833; ✉ 6C Sloane St., SW1, ☎ 020/7493–4232) was the first notable store to populate the South Molton Street pedestrian mall, and it seems to sprout more offshoots every time you see it. Well-established, collectible designers (Donna Karan, Romeo Gigli, Jasper Conran) rub shoulder pads here with younger, funkier names (Dries Van Noten, Jean Paul Gaultier, Hussein Chalayan). And if you want an Alexander McQueen/Givenchy, this is the place. Its July and January sales are famed. The **Hat Shop** (✉ 14 Lamb St., E1, ☎ 020/7247–1120) has long since moved from its Covent Garden base, but it's worth the trip (to trendy Spitalfields market place) for the huge range of hats, from everyday street style to something more wild or elegant, from £20. **Jigsaw** (✉ 126–127 New Bond St., W1, ☎ 0171/491–4484) is popular for its separates, which don't sacrifice quality for fashion, are reasonably priced, and suit women in their twenties to forties. **Jimmy Choo** (✉ 20 Motcomb St., SW1, ☎ 0171/235–6008) is the name on every supermodel's and fashion editor's feet. His exquisite, elegant shoes are fantasy itself but the designs aren't cheap—nothing under £100.

Koh Samui (✉ 65 Monmouth St., WC2, ☎ 020/7240–4280) stocks the clothing of around 20 hot young designers. Discover the next fashion wave before *Vogue* gets there. **Laura Ashley** (✉ 256–258 Regent St., W1, ☎ 020/7437–9760, and other branches) offers designs from the firm founded by the late high priestess of English traditional. **Selina Blow/Lulu Guinness/Camilla Ridley** (✉ 42 Elizabeth St., SW1, ☎ 020/7730–2449) are a co-operative group of designers whose designs are to die for. Guinness's prettiest bags and beaded party purses are must-haves; Blow tailors fine jackets, and Ridley completes the outfit with elegant velvet and floaty scarves. **Pellicano** (✉ 63 S. Molton St., W1, ☎ 020/7629–2205) stocks only cutting-edge designers, like Brit phenoms Bella Freud, Copperwheat Blundell, and Sonnentag Mulligan, and the Vogue-ier of the internationals (Prada). **Warehouse** (✉ 19 Argyll St., W1, ☎ 020/7437–7101, and other branches) stocks practical, directional, reasonably priced separates in easy fabrics and lots of fun colors. **Vivienne Westwood** (✉ 6 Davies St., W1, ☎ 020/7629–3757) is probably today's greatest British designer. Her Pompadour-punk ball gowns, Lady Hamilton vest coats, and foppish getups still represent the apex of high-style British couture. Her boutique is as intoxicatingly glamorous as her creations.

Department Stores

Harrods (✉ 87 Brompton Rd., SW1, ☎ 020/7730–1234), one of the world's most famous department stores, can be forgiven its immodest motto, *Omnia, omnibus, ubique* ("everything, for everyone, everywhere"), since it has more than 230 well-stocked departments. The food halls are stunning—so are the crowds, especially during the post-Christmas sales, which usually run during the last three weeks of January. **Harvey Nichols** (⊠ 109 Knightsbridge, SW1, ☎ 020/7235–5000) is famed for five floors of ultimate fashion—every label any chic well-bred London lady covets is here. There's also a home furnishings department. It's also known for its restaurant, Fifth Floor. **John Lewis** (⊠ 278 Oxford St., SW1, ☎ 020/7629–7711) claims as its motto, "Never knowingly undersold." This is a traditional English department store, with a good selection of dress fabrics and curtain and upholstery materials. **Liberty** (⊠ 200 Regent St., SW1, ☎ 020/7734–1234), full of nooks and crannies, is like a dream of an eastern bazaar realized as a western store. Famous principally for its fabrics, it also carries Oriental goods, menswear, womenswear, fragrances, soaps, and accessories. **Selfridges** (⊠ 400 Oxford St., SW1, ☎ 020/7629–1234), London's mammoth version of Macy's, includes a food hall, a branch of the London Tourist Board, a theater ticket counter, and a Thomas Cook travel agency. **Miss Selfridge** (also on Oxford Street, east of Oxford Circus, and other branches) is its outpost for trendy, affordable young women's clothes.

Street Markets

Bermondsey is the one the dealers frequent for small antiques, which gives you an idea of its scope. The real bargains start going at 4 AM, but there'll be a few left if you arrive later. Take Bus 15 or 25 to Aldgate, then Bus 42 over Tower Bridge to Bermondsey Square; or take the tube to London Bridge and walk. ⊠ *Tower Bridge Rd., SE1.* ⊘ *Fri. 4 am–noon.*

Camden Passage is hugged by curio stores and is dripping with jewelry, silverware, and myriad other antiques. Saturday and Wednesday are when the stalls go up; the rest of the week, only the stores are open. Bus 19 or 38 or the tube to the Angel stop will get you there. ⊠ *Islington, N1.* ⊘ *Wed. 7–4 and Sat. 8–5.*

Portobello Market is the place where every visitor to London first heads. There are 1,500 antiques dealers trading here, so bargains are still possible. Nearer Notting Hill Gate, prices and quality are highest, with bric-a-brac appearing as you walk toward Ladbroke Grove and the flea market under the Westway and beyond to Golbourne Road for the bargains. Take Bus 52 or the tube to Ladbroke Grove or Notting Hill Gate. ⊠ *Portobello Rd., W11.* ☺ *Fruit and vegetables Mon.–Wed., Fri.–Sat. 8–5, Thurs. 8–1; antiques Sat. 6–5.*

INDEX

✕ = *restaurant*, ⊞ = *hotel*

NOTES

p.32   Covent Gardens - street performers
       Carnaby Street

       Portobello Road

NOTES

NOTES

NOTES

NOTES

NOTES

NOTES